Unplug:
A Guide to Digital Detox and Mindful Living

Written by Shwe Line
Published by Cornell-David Publishing House

Index

3. The Science Behind Digital Addiction and Its Impact on Well-being

The Science Behind Digital Addiction and Its Impact on Well-being

Understanding the Brain's Reward System

1. Start with a morning routine:

2. Practice mindful eating:

3. Take regular breaks from screens:

4. Incorporate mindful movement:

5. Mindful communication:

6. Perform daily tasks mindfully:

7. Mindful breathing:

8. Meditate before bed:

9. Participate in mindfulness workshops / programs:

10. Establish a personal mindfulness reminder:

Stop, Breathe, and Be Present: Mindful Moments Throughout the Day

Mindful Mornings

Mini-Mindfulness Breaks

Mindful Evenings

9. Creating Healthy Digital Habits: Setting Boundaries and Maintaining Balance

Setting Boundaries and Maintaining Balance

Establish Clear Boundaries

Actively Maintain Balance

Cultivate Mindfulness and Self-Compassion

Embracing a Balanced Digital Life

Creating Healthy Digital Habits: Setting Boundaries and Maintaining Balance

1. Establishing Your Digital Values and Priorities

2. Setting Usage Limits and Implementing Technology Breaks

3. Developing Mindful Consumption and Communication Habits

4. Fostering In-Person Connections and Nurturing Genuine Relationships

5. Embracing Digital Minimalism and Simplifying Your Online Life

Setting Boundaries and Maintaining Balance: A Holistic Approach to Digital Well-being

1. Introduction: The Need for Digital Detox and Mindful Living

Understanding the Digital Quicksand

Technology has rapidly woven itself into every aspect of our lives. What began as a tool for efficiency and convenience has now become our constant companion – as deeply ingrained in our daily routine as morning coffee or brushing our teeth. And while there was once a time when the digital realm was a compartmentalized part of our lives, today, most people cannot go an hour – let alone a day – without being connected. This shift towards a life that is perpetually plugged-in has slowly, insidiously created a landscape of digital dependence – one that we are only now starting to realize may be affecting our lives in far more profound ways than imagined.

For some, digital technology has indeed been a blessing – helping us find the information we need, connecting us to loved ones from afar, and offering us seemingly limitless means of entertainment. But as we head further down this rabbit hole, we are also discovering that there may be a dark side to our digital dependence. We are starting to see that the constant barrage of screen-time, notifications, and digital clutter may be having serious mental, emotional, and even physical consequences on the very users these devices were designed to help.

This book, *'Unplug: A Guide to Digital Detox and Mindful Living,'* is created as an antidote to the modern tug of war between our desire to live meaningful, fulfilling lives and the allure of the always-on, hyper-connected digital world. We will explore the reasons behind our digital fatigue and the underlying causes of our compulsive device usage, with all the associated drawbacks that come with it. Together, we will begin the journey towards taking back control of our lives, finding balance in the digital age, and experiencing the benefits of a mindful, unplugged existence.

Some key objectives that this book aims to address are:

- **Identifying the reasons for digital addiction**: Recognizing the psychological and social factors driving our modern-day device dependence and understanding how it has become so ingrained in our culture that we hardly recognize it as a problem.
- **Exploring the consequences of digital overload**: Analyzing the adverse effects of digital dependence on our mental well-being, emotional health, interpersonal relationships, and overall life satisfaction.
- **Creating a digital detox plan**: Outlining the different approaches to digital detoxification, tailored to suit varying levels of dependence, and providing suggestions for establishing healthy boundaries with technology.
- **Introducing mindfulness practices**: Including various mindfulness techniques, both formal and informal, which can aid in finding balance, enhancing self-awareness, and promoting overall mental and emotional health.
- **Incorporating digital mindfulness into daily life**: Sharing practical tips and strategies to help maintain a conscious and intentional relationship with technology, emphasizing the importance of cultivating mindful habits for sustainable digital balance.

As we embark on this journey, it is essential to understand that the goal of this book is not to vilify technology or demonize the digital world. Rather, the intention is to promote awareness and inspire critical examination of our relationship with technology. By doing so, we can develop sustainable practices to regain control and to optimally utilize the best aspects of our digital tools while minimizing the negative consequences they may have on our lives.

It is our hope that as we delve into the various facets of digital detox and mindful living, you will feel empowered in your journey, embracing the freedom and joy that can come from releasing the chokehold technology has held on your life. Welcome to the path towards greater peace, balance, and fulfillment. Welcome to 'Unplug: A Guide to Digital Detox and Mindful Living.'

The Modern Condition: Overstimulation and Disconnection

In today's fast-paced world, technology has significantly changed the way we live, work, and communicate. The digital devices we use on a daily basis, such as our smartphones, tablets, and laptops, have provided us with unprecedented access to information, entertainment, and social connections. While these advancements can be incredibly positive and beneficial, they have also resulted in a new and challenging set of problems for our mental and emotional well-being.

It's no secret that our society is more connected than ever before. We can communicate with friends and family from across the globe through social media platforms, video chats, and text messaging. On the surface, this increased connectivity appears to be a positive development - after all, who wouldn't want to stay in touch with their loved ones and be updated with current events and happenings around the world? However, beneath this layer of perceived global intimacy lies a stark reality for many individuals: a feeling of disconnection, loneliness, and detachment from both the physical world and genuine human interaction.

One of the primary reasons for this sense of disconnection is the constant bombardment of digital stimuli that we face every day. Our brains are wired to respond to new information, and with countless apps, notifications, and messages clamoring for our attention, it's easy to become overwhelmed and distracted. This constant state of overstimulation can lead to a variety of issues, including high levels of stress, anxiety, and depression.

Furthermore, our reliance on digital devices for interpersonal communication has resulted in a decrease in the quality of our relationships and face-to-face interactions. We may have hundreds of friends on Facebook and a bustling group chat on WhatsApp, but would we recognize the people behind the screens if we passed them on the street? It's these genuine connections, devoid of technology, that carry immense and underappreciated value in our lives.

Now more than ever, it's essential to recognize and address the potential negative impact that technology can have on our mental health, relationships, and overall quality of life. This is where the concept of digital detox and mindful living come into play. These ideas present an opportunity for us to evaluate our relationship with technology, reset our priorities, and invest in deeply meaningful connections, both with others and with ourselves.

Digital Detox

A digital detox is the intentional reduction or complete removal of electronic devices and digital consumption for a predetermined period. This practice allows individuals to distance themselves from the barrage of digital stimuli and focus on reconnecting with their surroundings, thoughts, and emotions. By giving ourselves a break from the constant noise of the digital world, we can improve our mental well-being, increase our focus and productivity, and reestablish the crucial balance that is often missing in our lives.

Some potential benefits of a digital detox include:

- Reduced stress and anxiety levels
- Improved sleep patterns and quality
- Increased focus and attention span
- Enhanced creativity and problem solving
- Improved physical health and wellness
- Strengthened personal relationships

Mindful Living

While digital detox focuses on temporarily removing digital influences, mindful living is a more long-term approach to achieving balance and well-being in our lives. Mindfulness is the practice of being fully present in the moment, aware of our thoughts, feelings, and sensations without judgment. By incorporating mindfulness into our daily lives, we can improve our emotional intelligence and our ability to handle stress, foster deeper connections with others, and cultivate a greater sense of self-awareness.

Some strategies for incorporating mindful living into your life include:

- Practicing meditation and deep breathing exercises
- Cultivating gratitude and expressing appreciation for the little things
- Engaging in activities that nurture your physical, emotional, and mental well-being
- Prioritizing face-to-face interactions with loved ones
- Setting boundaries for technology use and incorporating digital detox periods

The combination of digital detox and mindful living offers a viable solution to the challenges we face in our modern, tech-driven world. By committing to recognizing the need for balance in our lives, assessing our personal reliance on technology, and practicing mindfulness, we can rediscover the essential human connections that bring meaning and fulfillment to our lives.

The Overwhelming Influence of Technology in Our Lives

In today's fast-paced digital world, we are constantly connected and inundated with information. From the moment we wake up to the time our heads hit the pillow, we have access to an endless stream of information, entertainment, and communication. This constant connectivity has brought numerous advantages and opportunities, but it has also introduced new challenges to our mental health and overall well-being. As we navigate this digital age, it's becoming increasingly important to recognize the need for a digital detox and cultivate mindful living practices.

The Negative Impacts of Digital Overload

Technology has truly revolutionized our lives, but at the same time, our dependence on it has grown exponentially. Recent studies have shown that excessive screen time and constant connection to digital devices can lead to negative health consequences, both mentally and physically.

- **Mental Health:** Prolonged exposure to screens and digital stimulation has been linked to increased anxiety, depression, and stress levels. This may be due in part to the nature of social media, where we tend to compare ourselves to others, or to the overstimulation and constant bombardment of information.

- **Physical Health:** Excessive screen time can also have detrimental effects on our physical well-being. Spending many hours sitting at a screen can contribute to a sedentary lifestyle, which can lead to obesity, heart disease, and other chronic conditions. Moreover, staring at screens for long periods can strain our eyes, causing eye fatigue, dryness, and discomfort.
- **Sleep Quality:** Our exposure to screens, particularly late at night, can interfere with our natural sleep-wake cycle, leading to poor sleep quality and disturbed sleep patterns. According to studies, the blue light emitted by screens suppresses melatonin, the hormone that regulates sleep, making it difficult to fall asleep and stay asleep.
- **Relationships:** Constant connectivity can also affect our relationships with others. Instead of having meaningful face-to-face interactions, people often resort to texting or connecting through social media. This lack of personal interaction can result in feelings of loneliness and isolation, even though we're seemingly more connected than ever before.

Rediscovering Balance: The Digital Detox

To counteract these negative effects and regain balance in our lives, a digital detox is necessary. A digital detox is the intentional act of disconnecting from digital devices and limiting screen time, allowing our minds and bodies to recover from digital overload. It's not about completely abstaining from technology but developing a mindful and intentional approach to our use of digital devices.

During a digital detox, we unplug from our devices and engage in activities that nurture our well-being, enrich our relationships, and encourage personal growth. This can include spending time in nature, practicing meditation, engaging in creative pursuits, or simply having meaningful, uninterrupted conversations with loved ones.

Embracing Mindful Living

Mindful living is an essential element of a digital detox, as it encourages us to be more present and intentional with our time and energy. By practicing mindfulness, we can better manage our digital consumption and make more conscious choices about how we interact with technology.

Some key elements of mindful living include:

- **Setting Boundaries:** Establishing clear boundaries with our devices can go a long way in promoting healthier habits. This could mean setting designated times for checking email or social media, limiting screen time before bed, or scheduling device-free periods during the day.
- **Prioritizing Self-Care:** As we reduce our screen time, it's vital to nurture our physical, emotional, and mental health. This can involve exercise, creative hobbies, meditation, or other activities that support our well-being.
- **Cultivating Gratitude:** While it's easy to get caught up in the negative aspects of technology, mindful living also involves acknowledging the positive ways it enriches our lives. By expressing gratitude for the conveniences and opportunities technology provides, we can create a more balanced perspective.

In conclusion, integrating digital detox and mindful living practices into our routine can help us navigate the complexities of the digital age and reclaim control over our well-being. By being more intentional with our time, energy and attention, we can create a more balanced and fulfilling life in this constantly connected world.

The Digital Age and our Overdependence on Technology

The digital age has brought on a myriad of advancements that have undoubtedly made our lives more comfortable, interconnected, and efficient. However, this great feat for humanity has also introduced several challenges to our mental, emotional, and physical well-being. Our dependence on technology — smartphones, computers, and various gadgets — has altered the way we live, work, communicate, and interact with others, making it increasingly difficult to strike a balance between our digital and offline lives.

Receiving constant notifications, being ever-connected, and the widespread phenomenon of FOMO (Fear Of Missing Out) have led to a compulsive need to stay engaged with our devices, constantly checking and updating our statuses, emails, messages, and social media presence. This pattern leaves many struggling to find a healthy balance and perpetuates an unhealthy web of compulsive engagement with technology.

The Ripple Effects of Technology Overuse

Technology overuse doesn't just result in plummeting productivity and increased procrastination; its effects run deeper and can impact a variety of life aspects that are essential to our well-being.

1. **Mental health:** Being constantly connected through screens can heighten feelings of anxiety, depression, and loneliness. Comparing ourselves to others on

social media and seeking validation through 'likes' can negatively affect one's self-worth, exacerbate low self-esteem, and even lead to feelings of isolation from the real world.

2. **Physical health:** Hours glued to screens means hours of inactivity, and an inactive lifestyle can contribute to several health issues, including obesity, cardiovascular disease, and muscular-skeletal problems. Moreover, excessive screen time can cause detrimental effects on sleep, which in turn can have a snowball effect on our overall well-being.

3. **Relationships:** Our addiction to screens can create distance when we replace face-to-face communication with digital exchanges. This detachment from reality can make it more challenging to foster empathy, active listening, and quality relationships.

4. **Work-life balance:** Struggling to set boundaries and achieving work-life balance can lead to burnout, reduced efficiency, and eventual workplace dissatisfaction. Technology overuse thwarts our ability to disconnect from work obligations during personal time and to give our minds the break it deserves.

5. **Attention and focus:** Multitasking between different digital channels and devices can erode our capacity for focused attention. This scattered approach has a lingering impact on our ability to concentrate on tasks at hand, ultimately hindering our cognitive, academic, and professional performance.

Digital Detox and Mindful Living: A Potential Solution

The answer to these problems lies in realizing that we can thrive in the digital age while committing to the idea of digital detox and mindful living, where we consciously make an effort to disconnect from our devices periodically and engage in our real-world surroundings.

Digital detox is not about a complete rejection of technology, but rather the mindful integration of technology use into our daily lives. It's about setting clear boundaries, taking breaks from digital distractions, and prioritizing self-care and genuine connections with others.

By incorporating digital detoxes into our lives, we can begin to rebuild a sense of balance and create a space for mindfulness, reflection, and self-discovery. Mindful living requires being in touch with our inner lives, becoming present in and appreciating the current moment, and providing ourselves the opportunity to unplug from the digital world so that we can tend to our real-life needs, desires, and contemplations.

In the following chapters, we will delve deeper into the potential dangers of our digital lives and guide you in partaking in a digital detox by highlighting several practical methods, habits, and lifestyle adaptations you can incorporate to achieve a healthier relationship with technology. These changes will ultimately allow you to reap the benefits of the digital age while maintaining your mental, emotional, and physical well-being. Now is the time to unplug and step into a more mindful and balanced life.

1.1 Understanding the Digital World and Its Effects on Our Lives

As we entered the 21st century, our lives have increasingly become intertwined with the digital world; at times, it feels like we are living in a constant state of connectedness with our devices. Smartphones, tablets, and computers are part of our daily routine, offering us a plethora of information at our fingertips, enabling us to work more efficiently and stay connected with family, friends and colleagues all over the world. But while technology has undoubtedly changed the way we live and communicate, it is also fraught with potential dangers to our emotional, mental, and physical well-being.

1.1.1 The Digital Overload

In an era where we have limitless possibilities for communication and social interaction, it is astonishingly easy to lose ourselves in the digital world, leading to what can be termed as "digital overload" – a phenomenon marked by a constant inflow of information, the endless need to stay updated on social media, and an ever-growing list of unread emails. This digital overload has resulted in a constant feeling of stress, anxiety, and fatigue among both adults and children, leading to a sense of being overwhelmed by the digital avalanche that has seemingly taken over our lives.

The constant barrage of information and the need to keep up with all that is happening in the online world is not just mentally exhausting but can also leave us feeling emotionally unsatisfied. Studies have shown that unrealistic comparisons with others on social media platforms can lead to feelings of inadequacy and discontent, affecting our self-esteem and, in some cases, can even lead to depression.

Constant connectivity has also disrupted our sleep patterns, leading to insomnia and other sleep-related issues. The blue light emitted by screens suppresses the production of melatonin – the hormone that controls our sleep and wake cycles. As a result, sleep quality is diminished, leaving us feeling perpetually tired and unable to concentrate fully on the tasks at hand.

1.1.2 The Impact on Relationships and Social Skills

Our digital dependency has not only altered how we interact with our devices, but also with each other. Texting, emailing and instant messaging have significantly diminished face-to-face conversations – once the building blocks of interpersonal relationships. This erosion of personal communication has led to a society where individuals often feel disconnected and lonely, even when surrounded by people who are physically present.

Children growing up in the digital age are especially susceptible to this change as they have never known a time without constant connectivity. Consequently, they may lack essential social skills, such as empathy and the ability to hold a conversation, which are needed to develop and maintain healthy personal relationships.

1.1.3 The Need for Digital Detox and Mindful Living

With these alarming consequences now slowly coming to the fore, it has become essential for individuals to unplug from their digital devices and connect with themselves and the people around them. This is where the concept of "Digital Detox" – a period of disconnecting from digital devices with the intent of reducing stress and focusing on other aspects of life – comes in.

Establishing a well-rounded digital detox plan and incorporating mindful living practices into our daily lives not only aids in breaking free from the relentless grip of the digital world, but also fosters a more fulfilling relationship with ourselves, others, and the real world around us.

In the chapters that follow, we will discuss different methods of implementing a digital detox, such as setting boundaries for device usage and establishing routines and rituals that help reduce screen time. Furthermore, we will delve into the practice of mindful living, which consists of becoming more present, self-aware, and focused in every aspect of our lives.

This journey of digital detox and mindful living is ongoing; at times, it may be challenging, but the rewards of better mental, emotional, and physical health, coupled with improved relationships and an enhanced quality of life, make it well worth the effort.

Through the pages of "Unplug: A Guide to Digital Detox and Mindful Living", we hope to assist you in finding balance between the digital and real-world, encouraging you to embrace the art of disconnecting and reconnecting with what truly matters.

2. Understanding Digital Overload: Signs and Symptoms

2.1 Recognizing the Signs and Symptoms of Digital Overload

As our digital lives continue to increase in importance, it's necessary for us to learn how to balance our online and offline lives. One of the keys to doing that is understanding when you've reached the point of digital overload. Digital overload is a phenomenon in which an individual becomes mentally, emotionally, and/or physically exhausted due to excessive use of digital devices or online activities.

The signs and symptoms of digital overload can manifest in several ways, affecting not only our quality of life but also our relationships and overall health. To help you recognize the signs of digital overload in yourself and those around you, we have compiled a list of common symptoms below:

2.1.1 Physical Symptoms

- **Eye Strain**: Excessive screen time can cause dryness, irritation, and strain in the eyes. If you're experiencing these symptoms, it's important to take frequent breaks and practice the 20-20-20 rule (every 20 minutes, look at something 20 feet away for 20 seconds).
- **Neck, Back, and Shoulder Pain**: Constantly looking down at your devices can lead to poor posture, which can cause discomfort and tension in the neck, back, and shoulders.
- **Carpal Tunnel Syndrome**: Overuse of digital devices can strain the wrists and cause carpal tunnel syndrome, a painful condition caused by compression of the median nerve in the wrist.
- **Sleep Disturbance**: Frequent exposure to screens, especially close to bedtime, can interfere with sleep patterns, resulting in poor or inadequate sleep.

2.1.2 Emotional Symptoms

- **Anxiety and Depression**: Overreliance on digital devices and social media can contribute to feelings of anxiety and depression, as you may become overly concerned with maintaining your online image or trying to keep up with the lives of others.

- **Mood Swings**: Excessive use of technology can lead to irritability and mood swings, often stemming from overstimulation or lack of quality social interaction.
- **Decreased Self-esteem**: Constantly comparing yourself to others on social media or feeling that you're not living up to an idealized standard can lead to feelings of inadequacy and diminished self-esteem.
- **Sensation of Missing Out (FOMO)**: The fear of missing out on activities or experiences others are having can bring stress and anxiety, leading you to spend more time on your devices to stay updated.

2.1.3 Mental Symptoms

- **Reduced Attention Span**: Overstimulation from multiple sources of digital media can lead to difficulties in concentrating on tasks for extended periods.
- **Memory Issues**: Heavy reliance on digital devices may impair memory retention, as we're often not fully engaged in experiences when we're preoccupied with our devices.
- **Decision Fatigue**: Making choices in a world dominated by endless digital options can exhaust our mental capacities, leading to decision fatigue and an inability to think critically and make optimal choices.

2.1.4 Social and Behavioral Symptoms

- **Increased Isolation**: Excessive device usage can make it challenging to maintain meaningful relationships, leading to increased feelings of isolation and loneliness.
- **Dependence on Devices**: Relying on gadgets to cope with feelings of boredom or to escape from daily

stressors can lead to an unhealthy dependence, making it difficult to engage in activities that don't involve a screen.

- **Neglecting Personal Responsibilities**: When digital experiences become more important than personal responsibilities, it is a clear sign of digital overload.

Understanding these signs and symptoms is the first step toward intentional digital detox and mindful living. Knowing when you or someone you care about is experiencing digital overload paves the way to make beneficial changes in daily habits and create a more balanced, healthy lifestyle. Remember, the key is not to eliminate technology from your life completely but to establish a healthier relationship with it.

2.1 Recognizing the Signs and Symptoms of Digital Overload

Digital overload, also known as digital fatigue or digital burnout, is a contemporary phenomenon that affects a large number of people today. Before we discuss strategies to unplug and detox from digital media, it is vital to learn how to identify the warning signs and symptoms of too much digital media consumption. By understanding these signs, you can take better care of your mental, emotional, and physical health.

A. Physical Symptoms

These are some of the most common physical symptoms you might experience due to digital overload:

1. **Eye-strain and discomfort**: Spending extended periods of time looking at screens can cause discomfort, dryness, and strain on your eyes. This

condition is sometimes called computer vision syndrome or digital eye strain.
2. **Headaches**: Staring at screens for long periods can lead to headaches, migraines, or even the exacerbation of pre-existing headache conditions.
3. **Neck, back, and shoulder pain**: Remaining sedentary or maintaining poor posture while using digital devices can result in neck, back, and shoulder pain.
4. **Sleep disturbances**: Excessive exposure to screens, particularly before bedtime, can interrupt your sleep cycle, and may lead to insomnia or poor sleep quality.
5. **Carpal tunnel syndrome**: Repetitive motions like typing or swiping on your devices can result in carpal tunnel syndrome, a condition that causes hand pain, tingling, and numbness.

B. Emotional and Mental Symptoms

Digital overload can also negatively impact your mental and emotional well-being. Warning signs include:

1. **Anxiety and stress**: Constant connectivity and the always-on nature of digital technology can be a source of anxiety and stress. It can create a sense of urgency to always be checking messages and notifications, leaving you in a continuous state of strain.
2. **Depression**: Studies show a correlation between high social media usage and depression. Comparing one's life to the highlight reels of others can lead to a decline in self-esteem and increased feelings of self-doubt.
3. **Decreased memory and attention span**: Continuously switching between tasks and devices can affect your ability to concentrate on one task at a

time. Over-reliance on digital tools for memory can also impair your natural ability to recall information without assistance.
4. **Social isolation and loneliness**: Excessive digital media consumption often comes at the expense of face-to-face communication and can contribute to feelings of disconnection from others.
5. **Addictive behavior**: Constant access to information, entertainment, gaming, and social networks can fuel feelings of addiction, as the brain gets hooked on the small doses of pleasure generated by these activities.

C. Behavioral Symptoms

When digital overload goes unchecked, it can lead to various behavioral changes, such as:

1. **Procrastination**: Constant access to digital devices can make it easier to put off tasks in favor of checking social media or playing games on your device.
2. **Multitasking**: The lure of digital media can lead to multitasking behaviors, such as checking social media or email while working or even using your smartphone during conversations or meals.
3. **Neglecting personal responsibilities**: Addictive behaviors surrounding digital technology may cause you to neglect essential aspects of your life, such as relationships, work, or self-care.
4. **Impaired decision-making and problem-solving**: A constant influx of information and distractions can impair your ability to make complex decisions and to think critically about problems.

Conclusion

Identifying the signs and symptoms of digital overload is an important first step towards regaining control of your life and finding the right balance between technology use and mindful living. By becoming aware of how digital media affects your well-being, you can make informed decisions about when and how to unplug, giving yourself the space necessary for personal growth and self-reflection. In the following sections of this book, we will explore practical strategies for digital detox and mindful living that will help you to better manage your digital media consumption and create a more balanced and fulfilling life.

2.1 Recognizing the Signs and Symptoms of Digital Overload

Before diving into the practical elements of a digital detox, it is essential to explore and understand the signs and symptoms of digital overload. Knowing when you've crossed the line into unhealthy Internet usage habits will empower you to act accordingly and regain control over your digital life. In this subsection, we will break down some common signs and symptoms of digital overload, so you can evaluate your own relationship with technology.

2.1.1 Physical Symptoms

Digital overload can have a noticeable impact on your physical health. Spending excessive amounts of time staring at screens or engaging in repetitive motions can result in a range of physical symptoms. Watch out for the following:

- **Eye strain and discomfort**: Staring at screens for prolonged periods can lead to digital eye strain or *computer vision syndrome*. Symptoms include dryness, itchiness, and discomfort in the eyes.

- **Neck, back and shoulder pain**: Sitting for extended periods in front of your devices, especially with poor posture, can lead to musculoskeletal issues, including pain in the neck, back, and shoulders.
- **Hand and wrist pain**: Excessive typing or using a mouse can cause repetitive stress injuries to tendons, nerves, and other soft tissues in the hand and wrist. These conditions are collectively known as *cumulative trauma disorders* and include carpal tunnel syndrome, tendonitis, and tenosynovitis.
- **Fatigue**: Spending excessive amounts of time using your digital devices can lead to reduced physical activity and poor sleep quality, resulting in overall fatigue and lethargy.

2.1.2 Emotional and Psychological Symptoms

Digital overload doesn't just impact the body; it can also profoundly affect our emotional and psychological wellbeing. Some common emotional symptoms of digital overload include:

- **Anxiety**: The constant barrage of information, notifications, and perceived social obligations can leave you feeling overwhelmed and anxious.
- **Depression**: Spending too much time on social media, in particular, has been linked to feelings of inadequacy, social isolation, and depression.
- **FOMO**: Fear of Missing Out (FOMO) is a term used to describe the experience of feeling that others may be having more fulfilling experiences or engaging in more socially desirable activities, which can create a sense of anxiety and dissatisfaction.

- **Decreased self-esteem**: Comparing ourselves to others on social media and other digital platforms can chip away at our self-esteem over time.
- **Guilt and shame**: Time spent mindlessly scrolling, gaming, or engaging in other digital activities can lead to feelings of guilt and shame about unproductive use of time and the resulting neglect of other areas of life.

2.1.3 Cognitive Symptoms

Digital overload can also interfere with our cognitive functioning—our ability to think, learn, and problem solve. Watch out for these signs:

- **Decreased attention span**: The instant gratification provided by digital devices can contribute to a significantly reduced attention span, making it difficult to concentrate on tasks for extended periods.
- **Memory problems**: Our reliance on digital tools to store and recall information can lead to a phenomenon called *digital amnesia*, where we become increasingly reliant on external devices for our memory storage, leading to diminished capacity for information retention.
- **Impaired decision-making**: Constant exposure to information and the necessity to make split-second decisions when using digital devices can cause cognitive overload, impairing our ability to make sound decisions.

2.1.4 Social Symptoms

Our relationships and social lives can also suffer as a result of digital overload. Some common social symptoms include:

- **Social isolation**: When digital devices become a significant part of your social life, you may find yourself opting for online interactions rather than face-to-face experiences, leading to feelings of social isolation.
- **Neglect of personal relationships**: Time spent on digital devices can interfere with maintaining personal connections, leading to friction and dissatisfaction in relationships.
- **Communication issues**: Overreliance on digital communication can limit our ability to engage in meaningful conversations, contribute to misunderstandings, and negatively impact our interpersonal skills.

If you recognize several of these signs and symptoms in your own life, it may be time to take a closer look at your relationship with digital technology. While these symptoms may vary in severity from person to person, ultimately, the goal is to find balance and moderation in our digital lives.

2.1 Identifying the Signs and Symptoms of Digital Overload

Digital overload, also known as information overload or tech stress, is the feeling of being overwhelmed by the constant influx of digital information and the endless demands placed on our attention by technology. It has become increasingly pervasive in our daily lives, but most people don't recognize the signs and symptoms early enough to take preventive action. Understanding the common signs and symptoms of digital overload is the first step toward addressing it and reclaiming a sense of balance in our lives.

2.1.1 Physical Symptoms of Digital Overload

Digital overload can manifest itself in various physical symptoms, as the constant engagement with technology leads to strain in the body. Some common physical symptoms include:

- **Eye strain and discomfort**: Staring at screens for hours on end can cause what is known as computer vision syndrome or digital eye strain. Symptoms include eye discomfort, blurred vision, dryness or redness, and even headaches.
- **Neck and shoulder pain**: Hunching over laptops, tablets, and smartphones puts strain on the neck and shoulders. This poor posture can lead to chronic pain and even nerve damage in the long run.
- **Back pain**: Sitting for extended periods and poor posture while using electronic devices can lead to lower back pain and spinal issues.
- **Carpal tunnel syndrome**: Repetitive strain on wrists and hands from typing and scrolling can cause carpal tunnel syndrome, a condition characterized by tingling, numbness, or pain in the fingers and hand.
- **Sleep disturbances**: Excessive screen time, particularly in the evening or before bed, disrupts the production of melatonin, a hormone that regulates sleep. As a result, it can lead to difficulty falling asleep, staying asleep, or getting restorative, quality sleep.

2.1.2 Emotional Symptoms of Digital Overload

Digital overload doesn't just impact our physical health; it can also wreak havoc on our emotional well-being. Common emotional symptoms include:

- **Increased anxiety and stress**: Constantly checking messages, social media, and pinging notifications can lead to heightened anxiety and stress levels as it becomes difficult to relax and disconnect from the digital world.

- **Fear of missing out (FOMO)**: Being continuously connected can lead to an irrational fear of missing out on something important or interesting, causing anxiety and social pressure to keep up with the constant stream of information.
- **Mood swings**: Exposure to the endless barrage of information and emotionally charged content can lead to mood swings, making it hard to maintain a consistent emotional state.
- **Depression**: Studies have linked excessive internet use to depression, as constantly comparing ourselves to others via social media can lead to feelings of inadequacy and lower self-esteem.
- **Decreased emotional intelligence**: Relying on technology for communication can lead to a decrease in emotional intelligence, as we become less attuned to the emotions of others and struggle to express ourselves effectively in face-to-face interactions.

2.1.3 Cognitive Symptoms of Digital Overload

Our brains are not immune to the effects of information overload, and cognitive symptoms can result from excessive technology use:

- **Reduced attention span**: Repeated exposure to the fast-paced digital environment can lead to a decrease in our ability to concentrate and focus for extended periods.
- **Impaired memory**: The constant influx of information and reliance on technology for retaining knowledge can lead to a decline in our ability to remember and retain new information.

- **Multitasking addiction**: Juggling multiple tasks and continuously switching between devices and platforms can lead to a compulsive need to multitask, even at the expense of productivity and efficiency.
- **Decision fatigue**: As our brains are bombarded with endless choices and decisions due to digital overload, it becomes more challenging to make sound judgments and prioritize tasks effectively.

2.1.4 Social Symptoms of Digital Overload

Digital overload can also have negative effects on our social lives and relationships:

- **Social isolation**: Excessive technology use can lead to social isolation as people prioritize digital interactions over face-to-face relationships.
- **Decreased empathy**: When we depend on technology for communication, it can lead to impaired empathic skills as we are less exposed to non-verbal cues and authentic emotional expressions.
- **Inability to engage in deep conversations**: Constant exposure to shallow and brief digital communications can make it challenging to engage in meaningful, in-depth conversations with others.

Understanding the various signs and symptoms of digital overload is the first step towards taking action, setting boundaries, and reclaiming control over our digital lives. Recognizing these symptoms in ourselves and others enables us to cultivate healthier relationships with technology and live more mindful, balanced lives.

2.1 Recognizing the Signs and Symptoms of Digital Overload

When we are constantly connected to digital devices, we often ignore or overlook the negative impact it has on our mental, emotional, and physical health. It is essential to recognize the signs and symptoms of digital overload in order to take appropriate steps towards a healthier lifestyle. The following subsections detail some of the major signs and symptoms of digital overload, along with strategies to recognize and address them.

2.1.1 Mental and Emotional Signs

1. Increased stress and anxiety

Rapid consumption of information, constant distractions, and a never-ending sense of urgency and immediacy contribute to increased stress and anxiety levels.

2. Mental fatigue and burnout

Hours of screen time, along with incessant multitasking, puts a significant amount of strain on our cognitive functions, leading to mental fatigue and eventual burnout.

3. Diminished attention span

Our reliance on digital devices for distraction and entertainment has led to reduced focus and a diminished ability to concentrate on a single task for extended periods.

4. Emotional disconnection

Overuse of digital devices can lead to a lack of meaningful connections and face-to-face interactions with others, resulting in feelings of isolation and loneliness.

2.1.2 Physical Signs

1. Eye strain and discomfort

Long screen times expose our eyes to blue light, which may cause eye strain, dry eyes, and discomfort.

2. Poor posture and musculoskeletal pain

Hours spent leaning over laptops, staring down at smartphones, and hunching over tablets can cause poor posture and contribute to neck, back, and shoulder pain.

3. Disrupted sleep patterns

Exposure to blue light from screens suppresses melatonin production, which can lead to difficulty falling asleep, disrupted sleep patterns, and decreased sleep quality.

4. Reduced physical activity

An increase in screen time often correlates with a decrease in physical activities, contributing to a sedentary lifestyle and, consequently, negative health effects.

2.1.3 Social and Lifestyle Signs

1. Device-dependent interactions

Constantly checking and responding to notifications or messages during social interactions can exhibit a lack of engagement and hinder the natural flow of conversations.

2. Compulsive device checking

Feeling the constant need to check phones or other digital devices, even when not expecting any important messages, points to an unhealthy reliance on digital stimulation.

3. Fear of missing out (FOMO)

Constantly checking on social media updates and comparing our lives with others can lead to FOMO, causing anxiety, depression, and dissatisfaction with one's own life.

4. Escapism

Using digital devices to avoid unpleasant thoughts, feelings or situations could be indicative of digital addiction and an unhealthy reliance on virtual distractions.

2.1.4 Identifying Your Personal Warning Signs

In order to recognize and effectively address digital overload, it's important to identify your own personal warning signs. These may differ from person to person, but common signals include:

- Persistent thoughts about checking your devices
- Irritability or anxiety when you cannot access your devices
- Using your devices in situations where it's not appropriate or safe
- Neglecting personal relationships, self-care, or important tasks in favor of spending time on devices

Being aware of these signs and symptoms is the first step in curbing digital addiction and promoting a healthier, mindful lifestyle.

2.2 Strategies for Managing Digital Overload

Once you have identified the signs and symptoms of digital overload, it's time to implement strategies for reducing your reliance on digital devices and leading a more balanced life:

1. Schedule device-free time

Establishing specific times each day or week for device-free activities can help you disconnect and focus on other aspects of your life.

2. Set app limits on your devices

Utilize the built-in features of your devices or download apps to limit the time spent on social media sites, games, or other time-consuming activities.

3. Engage in regular physical activities

Incorporating physical exercise into your daily routine can reduce the negative health effects of digital overload and help you maintain overall physical well-being.

4. Practice mindfulness techniques

Learning and practicing mindfulness techniques, such as meditation, deep breathing, or journaling, can help alleviate anxiety, stress, and emotional disconnection caused by digital overload.

Remember, a digital detox is not about completely eliminating digital devices from your life, but rather about finding balance, fostering mindful living, and developing healthier relationships with technology.

3. The Science Behind Digital Addiction and Its Impact on Well-being

The Science Behind Digital Addiction and Its Impact on Well-being

Digital addiction, also referred to as internet addiction or technology addiction, is a relatively new phenomenon that has emerged as our society becomes increasingly dependent on smartphones, computers, and other electronic devices. This subsection will delve into the science behind digital addiction and discuss the impact of this growing issue on individual and societal well-being.

Understanding the Brain's Reward System

To understand digital addiction, we must first understand the brain's reward system, specifically the role of dopamine. Dopamine is a neurotransmitter that plays a critical role in reward-seeking behaviors and the overall sensation of pleasure. Dopamine is released in response to a range of stimuli – from food and drugs to social interactions – and helps us decide whether or not to pursue those stimuli again.

Many online activities, such as scrolling through social media, watching videos, or playing video games, have been engineered to deliver intermittent, unpredictable rewards, similar to the mechanism of slot machines in gambling. The result is that the brain's dopamine system is activated, reinforcing our desire to continue to engage in these activities. Over time, this can lead to digital addiction, which is sometimes referred to as an "online behavioral addiction."

The Impact of Digital Addiction on Mental Health

Digital addiction can have a substantial impact on an individual's mental health. Research has linked excessive internet use with a variety of psychological issues, such as anxiety, depression, loneliness, and attention problems. In addition to the direct consequences of digital addiction, numerous studies have reported that individuals who spend excessive time online may also neglect important personal, social, and professional responsibilities.

One of the main reasons digital addiction has such a profound impact on mental health is that it can create a negative cycle of reinforcement. For example, some individuals may initially turn to online activities as a way of coping with stress, loneliness, or anxiety. However, over time, their reliance on digital devices may make it increasingly difficult for them to disengage from these activities and address the underlying causes of their emotional distress.

The Impact of Digital Addiction on Physical Health

Physical health may also suffer as a result of digital addiction. Excessive use of electronic devices can lead to a sedentary lifestyle, resulting in an increased risk of obesity, diabetes, and cardiovascular diseases. Moreover, the constant use of smartphones and computer screens can adversely affect sleep patterns, leading to insomnia and a host of other sleep-related issues.

Considering the amount of time that many individuals spend on their devices, there is also growing concern about the potentially harmful effects of blue light exposure from screens. This type of light has been shown to suppress the production of melatonin, a hormone responsible for regulating sleep-wake cycles. Consequently, individuals who spend excessive time on their devices – particularly in the evening hours – may have a more difficult time falling asleep and maintaining good sleep quality.

The Role of FOMO and Social Comparison

Fear of missing out (FOMO) and social comparison are additional factors that contribute to digital addiction and its impact on well-being. The constant barrage of information and updates from our digital devices can lead us to feel as though we are constantly missing out on something important, driving us to check our devices more frequently and increasing our overall screen time.

Moreover, the curated images and lives portrayed on social media platforms can lead to unhealthy social comparisons, leaving individuals feeling dissatisfaction with their own lives. This relentless comparison of ourselves to others can result in feelings of envy, depression, low self-esteem, and even narcissism.

Mindful Living as a Solution

Alternatively, mindful living offers a solution to help break the cycle of digital addiction and its negative impact on our well-being. By being more mindful of our technology use, setting boundaries and limits, and prioritizing activities that promote mental and physical health, we can reclaim control over our lives and foster a healthier relationship with our digital devices.

In conclusion, understanding the science behind digital addiction – particularly the role of the brain's reward system – allows us to recognize the gravity of the issue and the potential consequences for our mental and physical well-being. By incorporating mindfulness and intentionality in our relationship with technology, we can disrupt the cycle of addiction, paving the way for healthier, happier lives.

The Psychological Roots of Digital Addiction

One of the main reasons digital addiction is so prevalent is because of the psychological mechanisms that underlie our use of technology. Understanding these mechanisms can give us a better grasp on how to regain control over our digital lives.

Operant conditioning and dopamine loops

Digital addiction can be partly explained by a psychological phenomenon known as operant conditioning, which is the process through which we learn to repeat behaviors that lead to rewards and avoid those that lead to punishments. The use of smartphones, social media, and other digital platforms has been designed to maximize the rewards we receive through this process.

The main neurotransmitter involved in the reward system is dopamine, which is released every time we experience a pleasurable sensation. This sensation can be as simple as receiving a 'like' on social media or as complex as completing a challenging task on a video game. Every time dopamine is released in our brains, we feel motivated to repeat the behavior that led to its release, creating a dopamine loop that can encourage digital addiction.

Many apps and platforms capitalize on this basic human tendency and are intentionally designed to trigger dopamine releases. The constant notifications, social validation, and the opportunity for endless scrolling all contribute to this cycle, drawing us deeper into the digital world.

Fear of missing out (FOMO) and social comparison

Another driving force behind digital addiction is the fear of missing out (FOMO). This phenomenon is characterized by the feeling that we are always one step behind our peers, constantly missing out on experiences or information. As a result, we feel compelled to constantly check our devices, seeking reassurance that we are in the loop.

Social media platforms play a huge role in exacerbating FOMO by allowing us to have a sneak peek into the lives of others. This sneak peek typically presents a curated and idealized version of other people's lives, which can then lead us to make unfavorable social comparisons. These comparisons can generate feelings of inadequacy, jealousy, and dissatisfaction with our own lives, contributing to the vicious cycle of digital dependence.

Hijacking our attention and cognitive resources

In an environment saturated with digital stimuli, our technology constantly competes for our attention. Attention, much like time, is a limited resource – we may not realize it, but every moment spent on technology is one that we cannot devote to something else.

Many digital platforms are designed to be as engaging as possible, encouraging us to multitask and rapidly switch our attention between different sources of information. This constant bombardment of information can lead to a phenomenon called cognitive overload, where our cognitive resources are drained, and our ability to focus, think critically, and make decisions is compromised.

The Effects of Digital Addiction on Well-being

Digital addiction, like any other addiction, has detrimental effects on our overall well-being. Some of the ways digital addiction can impact our mental, emotional, and physical health include:

Mental health effects

Excessive screen time and digital addiction have been linked to increased rates of depression, anxiety, and stress. These associations may be explained by the constant social comparisons on social media, the overwhelm from information overload, and the isolation that can develop as personal connections are replaced by digital ones.

Emotional well-being

Digital addiction can also influence our emotional well-being. By fostering feelings of inadequacy and FOMO, as well as creating a constant need for validation through likes and comments, digital addiction can decrease our sense of self-worth and emotional resilience.

Additionally, the constant distraction of technology can make it challenging to practice mindfulness, a valuable tool for emotional regulation and self-awareness. By keeping us constantly stimulated, technology can make us less attuned to our own emotions and hinder our ability to manage emotional experiences effectively.

Physical health effects

Spending countless hours in front of screens can take a toll on our bodies. Increased screen time has been associated with a sedentary lifestyle, leading to negative effects such as obesity, poor cardiovascular health, and the development of various other chronic health conditions.

Furthermore, the excessive use of technology, particularly before bedtime, has been shown to interfere with sleep quality and duration. Adequate sleep is essential for maintaining optimal physical and cognitive functioning, making this disruption especially detrimental to our overall health.

Conclusion

Understanding the psychological roots and potential impacts of digital addiction is an essential step toward adopting healthier and more mindful digital habits. Gaining insight into these aspects of addiction can empower us to make informed decisions about when, where, and how we choose to engage with technology.

By being aware of the dopamine loops, fear of missing out, and attention hijacking, we can be more intentional in creating boundaries and making choices that prioritize our well-being. Breaking free from digital addiction offers the opportunity to reconnect with ourselves, others, and the world around us, enriching our lives and enhancing our well-being.

The Neuroscience of Digital Addiction

Digital addiction is a growing phenomenon that has been increasingly impacting our well-being. It revolves around the compulsive use of digital devices such as smartphones, computers, and other gadgets, leading to mental, emotional, and physical disturbances. This subsection aims to shed light on the science behind digital addiction and its effect on our overall well-being.

The Dopamine Reward System

At the core of digital addiction lies the brain's reward system, specifically facilitated by the neurotransmitter dopamine. Dopamine is a chemical messenger that plays a crucial role in human motivation, reward, and pleasure-seeking behaviors. When we engage in a rewarding activity, such as eating a delicious meal, exercising, or receiving praise, our brain releases dopamine, which results in the experience of pleasure and motivates us to repeat the behavior.

Similarly, engaging with digital devices, social media, and other online activities releases dopamine in our brains, reinforcing the behavior and making it increasingly harder to resist the urge to use these devices. For instance, receiving 'likes' or notifications on social media, winning a level in a game, or obtaining new information through internet browsing can all trigger dopamine release, making us want more.

Moreover, digital devices are designed to keep us engaged with countless features that exploit the brain's dopamine-driven reward system. Infinite scrolling, autoplay, notifications, and variable rewards are examples of features that enable us to spend longer periods on these devices, creating a habitual cycle of internet and device use.

Digital Addiction and Negative Emotional States

The frequent, compulsive use of digital devices, especially social media, can lead to the development of emotional disturbances such as low self-esteem, depression, and anxiety. Comparing ourselves to others on social media, feeling the pressure to maintain a 'perfect' online presence, and being exposed to a constant barrage of negative news and conflict can all create a sense of worthlessness, loneliness, and isolation.

Psychologists also propose that social media could potentially fuel feelings of envy, jealousy, and resentment among users. When our daily activities are continually interrupted by digital distractions, we may miss out on opportunities for building meaningful connections, cultivating empathy, and enhancing our emotional intelligence.

The Impact on Cognitive and Executive Functions

Digital addiction can also adversely affect our cognitive functioning, including attention, memory, and learning. A constantly connected lifestyle leads to fragmented thinking, shallow processing of information, and heavily multitasking, all of which weaken our ability to focus and think deeply.

Chronic use of digital devices is also associated with impairments in essential executive functions such as decision-making, self-regulation, and impulse control. The lure of these devices often leads to procrastination and the inability to prioritize tasks effectively. Consequently, our productivity, performance, and overall quality of work take a significant hit.

Physiological Consequences of Digital Addiction

Using digital devices for extended periods can lead to a range of physical health problems. Poor posture, back pain, neck strain, and carpal tunnel syndrome are among the issues resulting from prolonged device usage. Moreover, excessive screen time can result in eye strain, headaches, and disrupted sleep patterns due to the harmful effects of blue light emitted by these devices. Sleep disturbance, in turn, contributes to poor mood regulation, impaired cognitive functioning, and a weakened immune system.

Furthermore, a sedentary lifestyle caused by excessive digital device usage can increase the risk of obesity, cardiovascular diseases, and other chronic health disorders. A lack of outdoor activities and limited exposure to nature can exacerbate these health problems, further impacting our overall well-being.

Conclusion

Digital addiction is evident as a significant concern for our society's mental, emotional, and physical well-being. The science behind digital addiction rests on the dopamine-driven reward system, which facilitates compulsive use of digital devices. The negative emotional states, hampered cognitive and executive functions, and physiological consequences demonstrate just how significantly digital addiction can impact our lives.

Understanding the science behind digital addiction is only the first step in addressing its impact on our well-being. It empowers us to better comprehend the behavioral patterns that lead to compulsive use of digital devices, allowing us to develop effective strategies to promote a more mindful, balanced lifestyle that prioritizes well-being over constant connectivity.

The Science Behind Digital Addiction and Its Impact on Well-being

Digital Addiction: The New Age Habit

In today's fast-paced world, technology has seeped into every nook of our lives, connecting and engaging us with others and boosting our productivity. It is not surprising that usage of electronic devices, especially smartphones and other gadgets, has skyrocketed in the past decade. At the same time, however, we have seen the rise of what can only be called an addiction to digital devices, affecting both physical and mental well-being. Many researchers now argue that digital addiction should be seen as a genuine psychological disorder, deeply impacting our lives negatively. In this subsection, we will delve into the science behind digital addiction and explore its effects on our overall well-being.

Mechanisms of Digital Addiction

Researchers have likened digital addiction to substance addiction, drawing parallels between the two with respect to brain function and neurochemical regulation. As with any addiction, the cycle of digital addiction starts with an initiation phase, where the use of the digital device or application might begin as a means of coping with boredom or as a cultural phenomenon. What starts as a mild curiosity quickly turns into a habit and escalates into a full-blown addiction.

Digital addiction uses the reward mechanism found in our brains, which is responsible for reinforcing behaviors that are pleasurable or advantageous. When we engage in enjoyable activities, our brains release a neurotransmitter called dopamine. High levels of dopamine in the brain's reward system cause us to feel pleasure, satisfaction, and motivation, literally rewarding us for our actions. Addictive substances, like drugs or alcohol, also stimulate the release of dopamine, causing us to desire them over time.

Similarly, digital addiction also hijacks the dopamine-reward system. As we receive text messages, 'likes', and comments on social media or beat levels of a video game, our brains release dopamine. This loop of pleasure and reward consistently causes us to reach for our devices, even when it's not in our best interest. The constant desire for a dopamine hit creates an escalating cycle of addiction.

Psychological Traits Linked to Digital Addiction

Some individuals might be more prone to developing digital addiction. Researchers have identified certain personality traits as factors that might put someone at a higher risk for digital addiction:

1. Impulsivity: Those who exhibit high levels of impulsiveness might find themselves more likely to succumb to digital addiction. Impulsive individuals might struggle with self-control and the ability to resist digital temptations.
2. Sensation-Seeking: People who thrive on new experiences and constantly seek excitement might find themselves more vulnerable to digital addiction. Their need for constant stimulation aligns well with the rapidly changing and customizable world of digital technology.

3. Emotional Dysfunction: People who experience depression, anxiety, or other forms of emotional dysfunction might turn to digital devices for comfort or distraction from their stressful lives. The digital world may temporarily alleviate negative emotions or uncomfortable situations, leading to overuse and addiction.

Additionally, individuals with a history of substance abuse or other addiction-related disorders might have a higher risk of developing digital addiction due to the commonality of the underlying mechanisms related to dopamine and brain reward systems.

Impact of Digital Addiction on Well-being

Digital addiction is not confined to isolated cases; it affects a large portion of the global population. Various studies have outlined how digital addiction negatively impacts physical, psychological, and social aspects of well-being.

Physical well-being: Excessive screen time strains the eyes, leading to digital eye strain or computer vision syndrome, causing dryness, redness, and blurred vision. Sleep quality is also negatively affected, as the artificial blue light emitted from screens suppresses melatonin—a hormone responsible for sleep regulation. Furthermore, sedentary behaviors, such as prolonged sitting while using devices, contribute to obesity and other health issues.

Psychological well-being: Digital addiction assimilates symptoms of withdrawal, low self-esteem, mood disturbances, anxiety, and depression. Adolescents are especially vulnerable due to their higher likelihood of developing addiction to social media, video games, or other digital platforms, affecting their mental health.

Social well-being: Relationships suffer from digital addiction as it creates a sense of isolation by replacing face-to-face interaction with virtual communication. The addict often prioritizes digital devices over personal interactions or becomes preoccupied with them during social gatherings, leading to a decline in social skills and meaningful relationships.

Taking all of these factors into account, it becomes clear that digital addiction and its impact on well-being must be addressed. To break free from the cycle of digital addiction, we must become aware of our usage patterns and actively strive to create balance in our lives. Unplug: A Guide to Digital Detox and Mindful Living will provide you with practical tools and strategies to combat digital addiction and improve your overall well-being.

3.1 Understanding the Mechanism of Digital Addiction

The first step in understanding the complex nature of digital addiction and its impact on well-being is to identify the neurological and behavioral aspects that lead to the development of addictive patterns. In this subsection, we will delve into the science behind addiction, explore how digital addiction is similar to other types of addiction, and discuss the consequences of excessive use of digital devices and platforms on our mental, emotional, and physical well-being.

3.1.1 The Neuroscience of Addiction

Addiction can be broadly defined as a compulsive pattern of engagement in rewarding stimuli, which results in severe adverse consequences. Research has shown that addiction manifests changes in the brain's reward system, impacting various structures and neurotransmitters, primarily dopamine.

Dopamine, often referred to as the 'feel-good' neurotransmitter, plays a significant role in our brain's reward system. It gets released when we engage in pleasurable activities, such as eating, exercising, or using social media. Over time, repeated exposure to rewarding stimuli (such as drugs or excessive screen time) leads to changes in the brain's structure and functioning, resulting in increased cravings and an inability to resist the addictive behavior.

3.1.2 Developing Digital Addiction

Digital addiction shares several similarities with substance addiction. Both can lead to changes in the brain's dopamine-regulated reward system and are characterized by compulsive engagement despite negative consequences. However, digital addiction differs from substance addiction in that it involves the excessive use of digital technology, such as smartphones, social media, video games, and online shopping, rather than drugs or alcohol.

Several factors contribute to the development of digital addiction:

1. **Instant Gratification and Continuous Rewards**: Digital devices and platforms are designed to provide instant gratification, such as likes, shares, instant messaging, and notifications. This constant reinforcement creates a feedback loop that keeps individuals engaged and craving more, leading to a compulsive use of technology.
2. **Fear of Missing Out (FOMO)**: The pervasive nature of social media has given rise to FOMO, the anxiety

that arises from the belief that others might be having more rewarding experiences. This fear drives individuals to continuously check their devices for updates and spend excessive amounts of time online to stay in the loop.
3. **Variable-Ratio Reinforcement**: Digital platforms employ variable-ratio reinforcement, a schedule in which the reward is provided at unpredictable intervals. This element of uncertainty and randomness increases engagement and keeps users hooked, much like slot machines in casinos.

3.1.3 Impact on Well-being

Digital addiction can have far-reaching consequences on our mental, emotional, and physical well-being.

- **Mental Health**: Excessive screen time has been linked to increased rates of depression, anxiety, and stress. Research has found that individuals who spend more time on social media are more likely to experience negative emotions, rumination, and a decreased sense of overall happiness.
- **Sleep**: Digital devices emit blue light that can interfere with the production of melatonin, a hormone responsible for regulating sleep. Prolonged exposure to blue light, especially close to bedtime, can lead to sleep disturbances, difficulty falling asleep, and overall poor sleep quality.
- **Physical Health**: Sedentary behavior associated with excessive screen time can result in health issues, such as obesity, musculoskeletal pain, and increased risk of chronic diseases. Moreover, constant use of digital devices may lead to digital eye strain, resulting in dryness, pain, and discomfort.

- **Social Well-being**: While digital platforms can foster connections and allow us to stay in touch with our loved ones, excessive use of these tools may harm our social well-being. Online communication can lead to a decline in face-to-face interactions, feelings of loneliness, and issues with empathy, trust, and emotional intelligence.
- **Cognitive Functioning**: Over-dependence on digital devices can result in decreased attention span, impaired memory, and difficulty in problem-solving skills. The constant barrage of information and multitasking demands can lead to cognitive overload, making it harder for individuals to focus, process, and retain information.

In conclusion, understanding the science behind digital addiction allows us to recognize its impact on our well-being and empowers us to make informed decisions about our relationship with technology. As we continue exploring the principles of digital detox and mindful living, we will learn strategies and tools to break free from the negative effects of digital addiction and enhance our overall well-being.

4. The Art of Decluttering: Simplifying Your Digital Life

4.1 Evaluating and Reducing Your Digital Footprint

In today's digital age, we often amass a significant amount of digital clutter without even realizing it - and this clutter can have both tangible and intangible adverse effects on our lives. Just as a cluttered, disorganized physical environment can impede our ability to function effectively, a cluttered digital environment can negatively impact our mental state, work efficiency, and overall well-being. That's where digital decluttering comes in - assessing and reducing our digital footprint to create a digital environment that supports, rather than hinders, our mindful living goals.

Assessing Your Needs and Goals

The first step in the process of digital decluttering is to assess your needs and goals with respect to your digital life. Consider what purposes your current devices, platforms, and apps serve in your day-to-day life. Are they essential to your work, hobbies, or social life, or do they merely act as distractions that consume your time and energy? Are there any areas of your digital life that seem particularly prone to clutter or time-wasting? Having a clear understanding of what you need and value most in your digital life will guide you in eliminating the unnecessary elements, and retaining only the tools that contribute positively to your life.

Decluttering your Devices

Next, it's time to tackle the clutter that has accumulated on your devices over time. This includes the physical devices themselves (smartphones, tablets, laptops, desktop computers, etc.) as well as the software, apps, and files on them. To optimize your decluttering efforts, keep the following tips in mind:

- **Identify and remove unused or unnecessary apps and software:** Review the apps and software installed on your devices and identify any that you no longer use or don't find valuable. Uninstall them to free up precious storage space and reduce the visual and mental clutter associated with them.

- **Organize your files and folders:** Grouping similar files together, creating a clear folder structure, and deleting or archiving old or redundant files will make it much easier to navigate your digital environment and locate important documents, ultimately saving you time and energy.
- **Assess and manage notifications and communication tools:** Consider whether you'd benefit from adjusting your notification settings to minimize distractions during your focused work or leisure time. Also, evaluate which messaging or communication platforms are most essential to you and consider uninstalling, setting do-not-disturb hours or reducing notification frequency for the less important ones.

Taming Your Email Inbox

For many individuals, the email inbox serves as a major source of digital clutter - and consequently, stress. To address this issue, implement the following strategies:

- **Unsubscribe from non-essential newsletters and promotional materials:** Carefully consider whether each newsletter or promotional email you receive genuinely provides value to you, and if not, unsubscribe. This reduces the volume of emails filling up your inbox daily.
- **Establish a regular email management routine:** Make a habit of checking, sorting, responding to, and deleting emails at designated intervals throughout your day or week, rather than constantly reacting to each incoming message. This can help to minimize distractions and ensure that your inbox remains manageable.

- **Utilize email folders and filters:** Create folders and apply filters to organize your incoming emails, so that important messages are easily accessible, and less urgent or relevant emails are automatically filtered into designated folders for later review.

Streamlining Your Social Media Presence

For many people, social media platforms represent the ultimate digital time-sink and source of clutter. To address this issue, take the following steps:

- **Evaluate and prune your social media accounts:** Assess which social media platforms genuinely support your personal or professional goals, and consider deactivating, deleting, or significantly reducing your usage of any platforms that do not meet this criterion.
- **Curate your feeds:** Review the list of people, organizations, or pages you follow, and determine whether their updates align with your interests, values, or goals. Unfollow or mute any sources that contribute excessively to digital clutter or negatively impact your mental state.
- **Limit your consumption:** Schedule specific times for browsing social media, and set time limits for each session to ensure that you're not overindulging in unproductive or mindless browsing.

By taking the time to declutter and streamline your digital footprint, you'll not only create a more organized and efficient digital environment, but you'll also free up valuable mental resources that can be directed toward more mindful, fulfilling endeavors. So go ahead, start the digital decluttering process, and experience the myriad benefits of a simpler, more intentional digital life.

4.1 Embracing Digital Minimalism: Clear Out Old Files & Apps

What is Digital Minimalism?

Digital minimalism is the practice of intentionally simplifying your digital life by only keeping the essentials and removing distractions. When you declutter your digital space, you create more room for focus and mindfulness in your everyday life. A clean digital environment allows you to be more productive and intentional with your time, leading to overall increased well-being.

In the following subsections, we'll explore some practical strategies you can implement to simplify your digital life.

4.1.1 Delete Unnecessary Files

Regularly review the files stored on your devices to determine which ones are no longer useful or relevant. Make it a habit to delete duplicate files, outdated documents, and any other unnecessary files that have accumulated over time. This may seem like an insignificant task, but you'll be surprised by the difference it makes in terms of cleaner storage and a more organized digital workspace.

- Create folders and subfolders to categorize your files, and label them accordingly. This will make finding and organizing documents easier, and will help prevent excessive clutter in the future.
- Utilize cloud storage services, like Google Drive or Dropbox, for files that don't need to be stored locally on your devices. This not only helps keep your devices' storage clear, but also ensures that your files are accessible from any device with internet access.

Just remember to organize your cloud storage as diligently as your local storage.

- Regularly back up important files and documents to an external drive or cloud service. This way, if you ever need them, you'll have peace of mind knowing that they are safe and secure.

4.1.2 Uninstall Unused Apps and Declutter Your Devices

Take the time to examine the apps on your devices, deleting the ones you no longer use or those that only serve as distractions. A cluttered device is a constant source of distraction and can lead to increased screen time and digital fatigue.

- Assess the apps on your phone or tablet and delete the ones that don't serve a purpose or add value to your life. Be ruthless and only keep the essentials.
- Reorganize your apps on your home screen by categorizing them into folders or grouping them by function. This will make navigation easier and discourage you from mindlessly scrolling through endless pages of apps.
- Turn off non-essential notifications to reduce distractions and maintain focus. Research has shown that constantly receiving notifications can significantly increase stress and anxiety levels.

4.1.3 Email Management Strategies

A disorganized and cluttered email inbox can be a significant source of stress and disruption. By implementing the following strategies, you can simplify your digital life and improve your productivity:

- Establish a routine for checking and replying to emails at specific times throughout the day, rather than constantly monitoring your inbox. This can free up time for more important tasks and reduce unnecessary distraction.

- Utilize folders and labels to categorize your emails and make it easier to find specific messages. By sorting your emails into logical categories, you can expedite the process of managing and replying to messages.
- Regularly unsubscribe from newsletters, promotional emails, and subscriptions that no longer interest you or add value to your life. This will help keep your inbox clutter-free and reduce the amount of time spent sorting through irrelevant emails.

4.1.4 Social Media Detox

Social media can be a considerable time sink and contribute to feelings of digital overwhelm. Try the following strategies to reduce your social media consumption and cultivate a more intentional digital existence:

- Perform a social media audit by assessing the accounts you follow and removing those that no longer interest you or have a negative impact on your mental health. Be selective and only follow accounts that provide value, align with your interests or inspire personal growth.
- Implement a regular social media detox where you take breaks from social media platforms entirely. Use this time to focus on other aspects of your life, like personal development, hobbies or spending quality time with loved ones.
- Apply time management and mindfulness principles to your social media usage by setting specific times throughout the day to check your accounts, rather

than engaging in mindless scrolling during idle moments.

By embracing digital minimalism and applying the strategies outlined above, you can create a more peaceful, efficient, and mindful digital life, which in turn supports your overall well-being. Decluttering your digital environments allows you to reclaim your focus and prioritize genuine connections with yourself and others.

4.1 The Art of Decluttering: Simplifying Your Digital Life

Our modern lives have become overwhelmingly cluttered with digital information, notifications, gadgets, and tasks. The constant chatter of our digital lives leaves us feeling overwhelmed as we try to navigate this ocean of digital chaos. That's where the art of decluttering stands out as an essential skill. Digital decluttering is the process of simplifying your digital space to create an organized and peaceful digital environment – a space where your attention and energy are focused on things that matter most.

4.1.1 Identify Your Digital Clutter

The first step in the process of simplifying your digital life is identifying the sources of digital clutter. These can include:

- Emails, text messages, and chat apps
- Social media accounts, updates, and notifications
- Digital files, photos, and videos
- Apps, gadgets, and subscriptions
- Online articles, blogs, and websites
- Calendar events, to-do lists, and reminders

4.1.2 Prioritize Your Digital Needs

Ask yourself what digital tools, platforms, and resources are truly essential on a day-to-day basis. Write a list of priority items and compare it to the list of digital clutter you identified. This will help you notice the excess baggage you can do away with and focus on what's genuinely important.

4.1.3 Disconnect to Reconnect

Schedule regular digital detox sessions where you switch off all your electronic devices, including your smartphone and computer, and give your mind and body some respite. You'll be amazed by how recharged and focused you can feel after a digital break, and it will help you better connect with yourself and the people around you.

4.1.4 Tame Your Inbox

An overflowing inbox can lead to a dreadful sense of overwhelm. To declutter your inbox:

- Unsubscribe from newsletters and promotional emails that you don't read or need
- Create folders or labels to sort your emails by topic, sender or priority
- Use filters and rules to automatically manage incoming messages, like sending certain types of emails straight to a specific folder
- Set aside dedicated time slots during the day to check and respond to emails, instead of constantly checking them as they come in

4.1.5 Declutter Your Digital Files

A cluttered digital workspace can hinder your productivity and focus. To declutter your digital files:

- Create a clear and simple folder structure to easily locate your files
- Delete duplicate files and content you no longer need
- Regularly back up and save essential files in a secure cloud storage or external hard drive
- Rename files with descriptive names, so you can easily identify them

4.1.6 Streamline Your Social Media

Social media can be both a blessing and a curse, so it's crucial to be mindful of how you interact with these platforms. To declutter your social media:

- Limit the time spent on social media by setting specific time slots or using apps like Freedom or StayFocusd
- Unfollow, mute or hide accounts that don't bring value, positivity, or interest to your life
- Turn off or customize app notifications to reduce interruptions and distractions during your day
- Focus on interacting with people, sharing quality content, and nurturing relationships rather than accumulating "likes" or followers

4.1.7 Simplify Your Apps and Gadgets

An excellent rule of thumb is to only keep the apps and gadgets that you genuinely use, make your life easier or bring value to your life. To simplify your apps and gadgets:

- Delete unused apps and disable push notifications from non-essential apps

- Disable pre-installed apps that you don't use
  (bloatware), if possible
- Review the list of installed software on your computer
  and uninstall those you no longer use
- Consider selling or donating gadgets that you no
  longer need or use

4.1.8 Curate Your Digital Consumption

With the amount of information coming our way daily, it's
essential to be selective and intentional about the content we
consume. To curate your digital consumption:

- Use an RSS reader like Feedly or Inoreader to
  subscribe to your favorite websites, blogs or news
  sources, rather than getting lost in an endless cycle of
  aimless scrolling
- Create a bookmarks folder with your favorite articles,
  videos or other resources and set aside dedicated
  time to consume these valuable pieces of content
- Listen to podcasts or audiobooks that enrich your
  understanding or knowledge of a particular subject
- Be discerning with your choice of entertainment,
  opting for quality over quantity

By decluttering your digital life, you'll be setting the
foundation for a more intentional, mindful, and fulfilling
existence. Embrace the art of decluttering to achieve a
higher level of focus, calm, and clarity in all aspects of your
life.

4.1 Understanding Digital Clutter

Digital clutter is the accumulation of digital files, emails,
apps, and notifications that can overwhelm and distract us

from living a focused, productive, and mindful life. These digital items can easily take over our digital devices and spread into our personal and work lives, leaving us with scattered thoughts, less efficient in daily tasks, and lower overall mental well-being.

In a world where staying connected 24/7 is highly valued and digital noise is increasingly difficult to escape, it has never been more important to declutter our virtual spaces. Simplifying your digital life can decrease stress, increase focus and productivity, and improve overall mental health. In this chapter, we will guide you through practical tips and strategies to declutter and simplify your digital life.

4.1.1 Evaluating Your Digital Consumption Habits

The first step to decluttering your digital life is evaluating your digital consumption habits. Take some time to reflect on your daily interactions with your devices and consider the following questions:

- How much time do you spend on your devices?
- What activities are you engaging in? Are they productive or time-wasting?
- Can you identify any triggers that lead to excessive digital use or digital clutter?

Keep track of your digital habits for a week or two to gain a better understanding of where and how digital clutter is affecting your life. This can help you determine which areas of your digital life require the most attention and help you begin the decluttering process.

4.1.2 Tackling Your Inbox: Email Organization

Emails are a major component of digital clutter. Many of us receive hundreds of emails per day, making it difficult to keep track of important messages and stay organized. Here are some tips to help you declutter your email:

- **Unsubscribe from unnecessary newsletters and promotions**: Regularly evaluate the content you receive in your inbox and unsubscribe from anything that does not add value to your life.
- **Create folders or labels**: Use your email client's organizational tools to separate and categorize your emails. Some example categories include personal, work-related, finances, and subscriptions. This will make it easier to process and manage your inbox.
- **Establish a routine**: Set aside time each day to check and process your emails, ensuring that you stay on top of your inbox and avoid letting it spiral out of control.

4.1.3 Managing Files and Folders

Organizing your digital files and folders can save you time, improve productivity, and reduce stress. Adopt these habits to stay organized:

- **Create a logical file structure**: Organize your files into broad categories and then create subfolders to further break down your content. The key is to create a structure that makes sense to you and that you can maintain consistently.
- **Delete or archive old files**: Regularly review your files and delete or archive those that are no longer needed. This will keep your folders from becoming cluttered and help you stay organized.
- **Cloud storage**: Consider using cloud storage services to store and access your files from multiple

devices, as well as providing a centralized location to back up important files.

4.1.4 Streamlining Apps and Notifications

Smartphones and tablets often house countless apps and notifications that contribute to digital clutter. Take control of your devices by:

- **Deleting unused apps**: Remove any apps that you rarely or never use. This helps free up space on your device and reduces visual clutter.
- **Organizing your apps**: Organize the remaining apps into folders, grouping them based on their function or frequency of use. This will make it easier to locate apps and keep your device tidy.
- **Managing notifications**: Excessive notifications can be distracting and contribute to digital clutter. Review your notification settings and customize them according to your preferences, prioritizing those that are most important and disabling unnecessary ones.

4.1.5 Setting Boundaries: Detaching from Devices

Consider incorporating "device-free" periods into your daily routine as a way to take control of your digital life. Set guidelines around when and where you'll use your devices, and establish boundaries with family and friends. By limiting the amount of time you spend connected to your devices, you'll create more opportunities for meaningful and mindful experiences in your daily life.

4.1.6 Digital Detox: Taking a Break

Lastly, consider taking a temporary break from your devices, also known as a "digital detox." A digital detox can range from a few hours to a week or more, depending on your personal needs and goals. Setting aside time to disconnect will help you fully appreciate the benefits of simplifying your digital life and give you the motivation and clarity to maintain a decluttered digital environment.

By putting the above strategies into practice, you will notice an improvement in your mental well-being, productivity, and enjoyment for a more mindful and present life. We live in a digital age, and learning to declutter and simplify our digital lives is essential to finding balance, peace, and focus in our interconnected world.

4.1 The Importance of Digital Decluttering

In today's highly connected world, our digital devices have become an integral part of our daily lives. We rely heavily on smartphones, laptops, and tablets to work, communicate, and entertain. But the increasing reliance on technology and the internet has led to an unprecedented accumulation of digital clutter, which could harm our mental well-being, focus, and productivity. Digital decluttering is just as important as decluttering your physical space to create a more mindful and peaceful life.

4.1.1 How Digital Clutter Affects our Lives

Digital clutter can be anything from an overcrowded inbox, a torrent of irrelevant notifications, disorganized files, and folders, to a plethora of unused apps that consume storage space on your devices. Here is how digital clutter impacts different aspects of our lives:

1. **Mental Health**: Constantly engaging with digital devices and the stress of managing an overwhelmed digital space can lead to anxiety, stress, and sleep disorders. The blue light emitted by screens also plays a role in disrupting our sleep cycle.
2. **Time management**: Digital clutter makes it harder to locate the information or files we need, leading to wasted time and frustration. It also leeches valuable time through endless scrolling, procrastination, and multitasking.
3. **Focus and Productivity**: A cluttered digital workspace negatively affects our ability to concentrate and consequently results in decreased productivity at work or personal projects.
4. **Security and Privacy**: Disorganized digital spaces make it challenging to ensure privacy and may lead to security breaches like identity theft or data loss.

4.1.2 Steps to Simplify Your Digital Life

Now that we know why decluttering is essential let's look at the steps to take to start the process of simplifying your digital life.

1. Declutter Your Inbox

Email is often the primary source of digital clutter. To declutter your inbox:

- Unsubscribe from any newsletters, advertising campaigns, or notifications that you don't engage with or find irrelevant.

- Create folders for different types of emails (work, personal, finance, etc.), and use filtering rules to categorize emails automatically.
- Archive or delete old, unneeded emails.
- Set aside dedicated time slots every day to check and respond to emails to avoid constant email checking that hampers productivity.

2. Tidy Up Your Files and Folders

Organize digital files across all devices (computers, smartphones, tablets) following these steps:

- Create a simple, intuitive folder structure to group similar files together.
- Delete files that you no longer need, and back up essential files externally or on cloud storage for safekeeping.
- Use descriptive file names to make it easier to locate files in the future.
- Clean up your desktop screen regularly to maintain a focused workspace.

3. Manage Your Apps and Notifications

Examine the apps installed on your devices and remove any that you no longer use or find distracting. Customize app notifications and settings to prioritize those that are relevant to you.

4. Restrict Screen Time

Set limits on how much time you spend on your devices for non-essential activities like social media or gaming. Utilize the built-in screen-time monitoring features on your devices or use third-party apps to monitor your usage and hold yourself accountable.

5. Unplug Regularly

Create a routine of setting aside time for activities that don't involve digital devices like reading, exercise, or spending time with loved ones. Consider a digital detox, which can range from a few hours to a week or more, to reconnect with the offline world and give your mind and body a break from digital distractions.

4.1.3 Mindful Use of Technology

Digital decluttering is not only about removing excess from your digital life but also the mindful use of technology. Incorporate these habits for more intentional and mindful digital living:

- Prioritize single-tasking over multitasking to improve focus and productivity.
- Log out of social media accounts when not in use to reduce the temptation for mindless scrolling.
- Use Do Not Disturb or Airplane mode during focused work sessions, family time, or when you are unwinding for the day.
- Allocate specific times in your routine for checking social media or news updates to avoid being inundated by information throughout the day.

Ultimately, simplifying your digital life is an iterative process that requires regular maintenance and conscious effort. By decluttering your digital spaces, managing screen time, and adopting mindful habits, you can create a more focused, productive, and peaceful life, both online and offline.

5. Mindfulness and Meditation: Cultivating Inner Peace in a Connected World

The Benefits of Mindfulness and Meditation in a Connected World

In a world where the digital landscape is constantly evolving, it can be challenging to find moments of mental quiet and calm. The constant connectivity provided by smartphones, social media, and the internet can breed anxiety, stress, and a perpetual sense of distraction. While advances in technology have undoubtedly made our lives more convenient in many ways, they also have the potential to adversely affect our mental well-being. Therefore, turning to mindfulness and meditation practices can prove to be an essential tool in regaining balance, fostering mental clarity, and cultivating inner peace.

Understanding Mindfulness

At its core, mindfulness is the practice of becoming more aware of the present moment, without judgment. This heightened awareness extends to your thoughts, emotions, bodily sensations, and environment. By cultivating mindfulness, you can learn to respond to your thoughts and emotions more consciously, rather than simply reacting out of habit or autopilot.

Meditation as a Practice for Mindfulness

Meditation is one of the most effective ways to develop mindfulness. There are many forms of meditation, but most involve some combination of focused attention, open awareness, and a non-judgmental attitude. A regular meditation practice can help train the mind to be present, less reactive, and better equipped to manage the constant stream of stimuli offered by our digital world.

The Digital Detox: Reconnecting to Yourself and the World

One effective method of incorporating mindfulness and meditation into your life is by periodically engaging in a digital detox. By turning off your devices, disconnecting from social media, and setting aside dedicated time for quiet reflection, you can create an environment that is more conducive to mindfulness and meditation.

A digital detox does not necessarily mean completely renouncing technology. Instead, it involves carving out specific times and spaces in your daily routine to be device-free. This can be as simple as designating the first and last 30 minutes of every day to be tech-free, or as involved as planning a weekend retreat dedicated to mindfulness and reconnecting with nature.

Mindfulness Practices for Everyday Life

In addition to formal meditation sessions, there are many everyday activities that can help cultivate mindfulness. These practices can be easily integrated into your daily routine, even in the midst of a busy, digital-dominated lifestyle.

1. *Mindful Eating*: Eating slowly and mindfully not only improves digestion but can also be an exercise in mindfulness. By focusing on the taste, texture, and aroma of each bite, you can bring awareness to the present moment and experience a greater sense of satisfaction and enjoyment from your meals.
2. *Walking Meditation*: Walking can provide an opportunity to practice mindfulness and meditation. As you walk, focus your attention on the sensation of your feet touching the ground or on your breathing. This can help cultivate a sense of presence and awareness to the present moment.
3. *Deep Breathing Exercises*: Deep, slow breaths help activate the body's parasympathetic nervous system, which counteracts the stress response. By intentionally focusing on your breath whenever you feel stressed or overwhelmed, you can bring a moment of mindfulness and respite into your day.
4. *Gratitude Journaling*: Keeping a gratitude journal can help direct your attention toward the positive aspects of your life. This practice can train the mind to look for things to be grateful for, which in turn promotes a sense of happiness and contentment.

Letting Go of the Need for Constant Connectivity

Ultimately, incorporating mindfulness and meditation practices into your life is an essential step in letting go of the incessant need for digital engagement. By dedicating specific times and spaces for introspection and disconnection, you can establish a healthier relationship with technology – one that allows you to thrive in your digital life without feeling overwhelmed by it.

Remember that mindfulness and meditation are not meant to be a rigid regimen but rather a flexible set of tools that can be adapted to your individual needs and lifestyle. Embracing a digital detox and a mindful existence in our connected world can help foster greater mental clarity, inner peace, and overall well-being.

5. Mindfulness and Meditation: Cultivating Inner Peace in a Connected World

In this digital age, our lives are continuously interwoven with technology. Smartphones, social media, email, and countless other platforms facilitate our constant connection to the virtual world. While these tools certainly have their benefits, they can also contribute to feelings of stress, anxiety, and disconnection from our inner selves. As a result, mindfulness and meditation have emerged as vital practices for those seeking to restore balance and promote inner peace in an increasingly connected world.

5.1 Understanding Mindfulness and Meditation

At their core, mindfulness and meditation are practices that encourage present-moment awareness and foster a deep connection with the self.

Mindfulness is the practice of consciously directing your attention to the present moment, while maintaining a non-judgmental and open-minded attitude. This practice encourages individuals to observe their thoughts, feelings, and bodily sensations without getting caught up in judgments or evaluations. The goal of mindfulness is to cultivate greater self-awareness and develop a more compassionate relationship with oneself and the world.

Meditation is a complementary practice to mindfulness that involves setting aside dedicated time to focus on and develop awareness of a particular object, sensation, or mental process. Meditation can take many forms, such as breath awareness, loving-kindness meditation, or guided visualization. The purpose of meditation is to train the mind to maintain focus and clarity, while fostering a sense of inner tranquility and equanimity.

5.2 Incorporating Mindfulness and Meditation Into Your Digital Detox

Integrating mindfulness and meditation into your digital detox is an effective way to counteract the tendency to get lost in the virtual world and reclaim your sense of inner peace. Here are some ways to incorporate these practices into your daily life:

- **Start Small:** Begin by setting aside just a few minutes each day for mindfulness or meditation practice. Gradually increase the duration as you become more comfortable with the techniques and start to experience the benefits.
- **Create a Meditation Space:** Designate a quiet, comfortable area in your home as your meditation space. This could be a corner of your bedroom, a spot on your living room floor, or even a cushion near a window. Having a dedicated space for meditation will make it easier to establish a consistent practice.
- **Implement Mindful Breaks:** Make it a habit to take regular breaks throughout the day to quiet your mind and focus on your breath. This could be as simple as pausing at your desk for a few deep breaths, or taking a short walk outside to reconnect with nature.
- **Limit Screen Time:** One of the main goals of a digital detox is to reduce exposure to screens and digital

devices. Establish boundaries around your technology use, such as avoiding screens immediately before bed or setting aside specific times for checking email and social media.

- **Explore Different Meditation Techniques:** There are countless meditation methods and techniques available, so don't be afraid to explore different options to find the one that resonates with you. Some popular methods include mindful breathing, body scans, and walking meditation.
- **Join a Meditation Group or Class:** Practicing meditation with others can be a helpful way to stay accountable and deepen your practice. Seek out local meditation groups or attend a class at your local yoga studio.

5.3 The Benefits of Mindfulness and Meditation in a Connected World

The practice of mindfulness and meditation offers a myriad of benefits that can counterbalance the challenges of the digital age, including:

- **Reduced Stress and Anxiety:** Numerous studies have shown that mindfulness and meditation practices can lead to lower levels of stress and anxiety, as well as promote emotional stability and resilience.
- **Improved Focus and Concentration:** Developing present-moment awareness through meditation trains the mind to be more focused and less prone to distraction, which is an invaluable skill in an era of constant digital connection.
- **Greater Self-Awareness:** Through consistent mindfulness practice, individuals may experience increased self-awareness and greater emotional

intelligence, empowering them to make more informed decisions and respond effectively to challenging situations.
- **Enhanced Creativity and Problem Solving:** Many people report experiencing greater creativity and an increased ability to think "outside the box" following a meditation or mindfulness session.
- **Deeper Connection to the Present Moment:** Cultivating an appreciation for the present moment can help individuals feel less overwhelmed by the rapid pace of the digital world and genuinely connect with the experiences and people in their lives.

By integrating mindfulness and meditation into your digital detox, you can regain control over your technology use, and foster a greater sense of inner peace and harmony. The result is a more balanced and fulfilling existence in our fast-paced, connected world.

5.1 The Importance of Mindfulness and Meditation in a Digital Age

5.1.1 Why Mindfulness and Meditation Matter

In the era of constant connectivity, our minds are persistently bombarded with an endless stream of information, notifications, and digital distractions. While these advances have provided unparalleled convenience and access to information, they have also led to an insidious effect on our mental health and overall quality of life. The necessity for mindfulness and meditation in today's digital age has never been more important, as both practices offer an accessible and effective means to regain balance and inner peace amidst the chaos.

Mindfulness, at its core, is about awareness and presence. It's about being fully aware of your thoughts, emotions, and the sensations in your body as they all arise, without distraction or judgement. This present-moment awareness enables you to cultivate a deeper connection with yourself and truly experience each aspect of your life, free from the noise and clutter that so often pervades our everyday existence in a digitally dominated world.

Similarly, meditation is a profound practice that transcends time and religious conventions. Rooted in ancient wisdom, this practice has widely been recognized for its remarkable impact on mental and physiological wellbeing. The primary goal of meditation is to achieve deep relaxation and a focused, untroubled mental state by training the mind to become still and focused, even amidst chaos and disturbance.

5.1.2 Practices to Unplug and Cultivate Inner Peace

Reclaiming inner peace in a connected world is possible, despite the prevalence of digital distractions, through the regular practice of mindfulness and meditation. Here are some effective methods to incorporate into your daily life, allowing balance and tranquility to prevail:

1. **Intentional Digital Detox**: Set aside specific times and periods to unplug from digital devices, and intentionally focus on other activities to immerse yourself in fully – be it reading, cooking, or spending time with loved ones. This conscious effort to disconnect cultivates mindfulness by enabling you to be fully present in each undertaking, free from the distractions that so often permeate our daily experiences.

2. **Mindful Breathing**: Bring your attention to your breath throughout the day, particularly when feeling overwhelmed or facing the onslaught of digital distractions. Calm and steady inhalations and exhalations can help anchor you in the present moment, providing a refuge from external chaos and grounding you in a state of inner peace.

3. **Body Scans**: Periodically, check in with your body to notice any signs of tension or discomfort, and use this awareness as a cue to release any physical or cognitive strain. By regularly engaging in body scans, you not only promote relaxation but also become more in tune with the subtle changes in your body, fostering a holistic approach to inner peace.

4. **Meditation**: Engage in regular meditation, starting with just a few minutes each day and gradually increasing the duration as you become more comfortable with the practice. There are countless meditation techniques you can explore, from simply observing your breath to pursuing more structured practices such as loving-kindness or guided imagery meditations. Whatever your preference, the consistent practice of meditation will improve your ability to notice and navigate digital distractions, enabling you to stay focused and relaxed even amid the clamor.

5. **Nature Immersion**: Make time to spend in nature, away from the hustle and bustle of modern life. This could involve going for a walk in the park or planning a weekend getaway in a serene natural setting. The tranquility and beauty of nature have a soothing effect on our minds, helping to mitigate the adverse effects of perpetual connectivity.

5.1.3 The Benefits of a Mindful and Meditative Lifestyle

By integrating mindfulness and meditation into your life, you can experience a myriad of benefits that extend well beyond counteracting the effects of digital overload:

- **Reduced stress and anxiety**: Mindfulness and meditation practices are widely recognized for their powerful stress-relieving properties, as they naturally encourage the release of tension and restoration of peace within the body and the mind.
- **Enhanced focus and concentration**: These practices require the development and refinement of the skill to sustain focused attention on a single point, be it the breath, a mantra, or a specific sensation in the body. As a result, you'll experience increased mental clarity and the ability to concentrate on tasks and responsibilities with greater ease.
- **Increased self-awareness**: As present-moment awareness deepens, so too does your connection with yourself. This enhanced self-awareness will empower you with a deeper understanding of your thought patterns, emotional triggers and unconscious habits, allowing you to cultivate healthier, more intentional behaviors.
- **Greater emotional resilience**: With regular mindfulness and meditation practice, you'll develop an increased capacity to navigate challenging emotions and situations skillfully, enabling resilience in the face of adversity.
- **Improved physical health**: Research has shown that these practices have a remarkable impact on physical health, ranging from reduced cortisol levels and lower blood pressure to enhanced immunity and healthier sleep patterns.

In conclusion, as modern society continues its rapid technological advancements, it becomes increasingly essential to prioritize mindfulness and meditation amidst the digital chaos. By dedicating time to unplug and cultivate inner peace, we not only equip ourselves with the tools to navigate digital distractions skillfully, but also unveil a deeper connection with ourselves and our world.

5.1 Understanding Mindfulness and Meditation in a Digital World

In today's world, we are continuously drowning in an ocean of digital gadgets, social media notifications, and work emails. As we become more and more attached to our devices, it can be incredibly challenging to find inner peace and stay connected to the present moment. Excessive use of technology takes a toll on our mental focus, physical health, and emotional well-being. We constantly feel an urge to check our phones, even when there is no new message or notification. This obsession has made it more critical than ever to incorporate mindfulness and meditation in our lives to better navigate the connected world.

What is Mindfulness?

Mindfulness is a mental state achieved by focusing on the present moment while calmly acknowledging and accepting your feelings, thoughts, and bodily sensations without judgment. It involves paying attention to the process rather than the content of our experiences. By being fully present in the moment, we can live with more awareness, understanding, and inner peace.

What is Meditation?

Meditation is a practice where individuals use specific techniques like focusing on their breath or mental visualization to achieve a mentally clear and emotionally calm state. It involves training the mind to develop concentration, clarity, emotional positivity, and a calm view of the true nature of things. Meditation can last for several minutes to hours, depending on individual preference and comfort.

The Connection Between Mindfulness and Meditation

Mindfulness and meditation are interconnected practices that help cultivate inner peace, self-awareness, and emotional balance. While mindfulness is a state of being, meditation is an activity that helps to achieve that state. Practicing mindfulness meditation can assist you in developing a mindful approach to everyday life, enabling you to break free from the constant pull of digital distractions and live in the present moment.

5.2 Benefits of Mindfulness and Meditation in the Digital Age

1. **Increased self-awareness**: By learning to pay attention to your thoughts, feelings, and physical sensations, you can become more aware of your inner state and gain insights into your emotional patterns. Mindfulness and meditation help you recognize and change negative thinking patterns, improving your emotional well-being.
2. **Reduced stress and anxiety**: The constant bombardment of digital stimuli takes a toll on our stress levels. Practicing mindfulness meditation reduces stress by activating the parasympathetic nervous system, which helps you enter a relaxed state. By learning to focus on your breath, you can

turn your attention away from anxious thoughts and gain control over your emotions.

3. **Improved focus and concentration**: The continuous flow of notifications, messages, and information from multiple digital sources can fragment our focus and make it difficult to concentrate on important tasks. Practicing mindfulness and meditation helps you regain control over your attention, leading to improved productivity and concentration on tasks at hand.

4. **Enhanced emotional intelligence**: Mindfulness and meditation allow you to observe your thoughts and emotions without reacting to them impulsively. This helps you develop a keen sense of emotional awareness and empathy toward yourself and others, improving interpersonal relationships in both personal and professional spheres.

5. **Balanced use of technology**: Incorporating mindfulness meditation into your life can help you develop a healthier relationship with technology. As you become more aware of your thoughts and actions, you can make conscious choices about when to engage with digital devices and when to step away, leading to a more mindful use of technology.

5.3 Mindfulness and Meditation Techniques for Digital Detox

5.3.1 Mindful Breathing

One of the simplest and most effective mindfulness meditation techniques is mindful breathing. This practice involves focusing your attention on your breath as it flows in and out of your body. Use the following steps to practice mindful breathing:

- Find a quiet and comfortable place to sit in an upright position with a straight back.
- Close your eyes and take a few deep breaths, inhaling slowly through your nose and exhaling through your mouth.
- Shift your focus to your natural breathing pattern, observing the movement of your chest, rib cage, and diaphragm as you breathe.
- If your mind wanders, gently bring your focus back to your breath without judgment.
- Practice for 5-10 minutes, gradually increasing the duration as you become more comfortable with the practice.

5.3.2 Body Scan Meditation

Body scan meditation is a mindfulness technique that involves paying attention to different parts of your body in a systematic manner. This technique increases awareness of bodily sensations, promotes relaxation, and can be a helpful practice before bedtime. To practice body scan meditation:

- Lie down on your back in a comfortable position.
- Starting with your feet and moving up through your body, bring your attention to each part of your body in turn.
- Acknowledge any sensations or tension without judgment and let it go, allowing relaxation to take its place.
- Spend some time on each body part before moving to the next, working your way up to the top of your head.
- Once you've completed scanning your entire body, bring your focus back to your breath for a few moments before ending the meditation.

5.3.3 Mindful Device Usage

As digital technology is an inevitable part of our lives, it's essential to develop mindful habits when using digital devices. Here are some tips for mindful device usage:

- Set designated times for checking emails and social media accounts, instead of responding to every notification as it comes.
- Be fully present during your social interactions, whether in-person or virtual, by putting your devices away and giving your complete attention to the person you are with.
- Establish tech-free zones and times, such as during meals or before bedtime, to create routine periods of disconnection from digital distractions.
- Use apps that track and limit screen time or encourage meditation and mindfulness, like Headspace, Calm, or Moment, to support your digital detox journey.

Incorporating mindfulness and meditation practices into your daily routine can help you cultivate inner peace and a balanced relationship with technology. Be patient and gentle with yourself throughout your journey, and remember that the ultimate goal is to live a more connected, present, and meaningful life.

Mindfulness and Meditation: Cultivating Inner Peace in a Connected World

Introduction: A World of Distractions

In today's hyperconnected world, distractions surround us in the form of notifications, emails, social media, and news updates. While these technological advancements provide convenience and help us stay connected, it's easy for the mind to get overwhelmed, anxious, and lose touch with the essential inner peace and focus that we need to thrive.

Now more than ever, sustainable well-being is rooted in the ability to cultivate mindfulness and inner peace even within our connected lives. In this increasingly busy world, we must learn to train our minds to focus, manage stress, and maintain balance by incorporating mindful practices such as meditation into our daily lives.

What is Mindfulness?

Mindfulness is a mental state achieved by intentionally directing your attention and awareness to the present moment, calmly acknowledging and accepting your feelings, thoughts, and bodily sensations. The ultimate goal is to cultivate a non-judgmental awareness of the happenings within and around us simultaneously.

Using mindfulness, we can reduce automatic negative thoughts and reactions, increase self-awareness, and focus on the present moment. This centered state of mind helps to improve emotional and mental well-being, making us more resilient in overcoming life's challenges.

Meditation: A Tool for Cultivating Mindfulness

Meditation is an ancient practice that has been used for centuries to cultivate mindfulness by fostering focused, non-judgmental awareness of the present moment. There are various types of meditation, including:

1. **Focused Attention Meditation**: During this type of meditation, the practitioner concentrates on a single point of focus, such as their breath, a mantra or

sound, or a visual object. As the attention drifts away from the focal point, the practitioner must gently bring it back without judgment.

2. **Body Scan Meditation**: This type of meditation involves bringing your attention to each part of your body, starting from your toes and moving up to your head, observing any sensations or tensions present without judgment.

3. **Loving-Kindness Meditation**: This meditation encourages practitioners to cultivate feelings of compassion and love for themselves, loved ones, strangers, and even enemies. It involves focusing the mind on nurturing positive emotions and directing them towards others.

4. **Mindfulness-Based Stress Reduction (MBSR)**: Developed by Jon Kabat-Zinn, MBSR is an eight-week program that combines mindfulness meditation, body-awareness practices, and yoga. MBSR has been shown to improve mental well-being, decrease stress levels, and increase overall life satisfaction.

By practicing meditation regularly, one can strengthen their mindfulness muscle and effectively quiet the mental noise that contributes to stress, anxiety, and other negative emotions.

Tips for Incorporating Mindfulness and Meditation into Your Daily Routine

It can seem daunting to integrate mindfulness and meditation into an already busy schedule. However, remember that even a few minutes each day can bring remarkable benefits. Here are some tips to help you build a sustainable practice.

1. **Start small**: Aim to meditate for just a few minutes per day, gradually increasing the duration over time. You can use guided meditation apps or attend local classes to help initially.
2. **Create a routine**: Incorporate meditation into your daily routine, ideally at the same time each day. It could be right after waking up, during lunchtime, or before bedtime.
3. **Designate a meditation space**: Create a comfortable, tranquil space for your meditation practice. You could use cushions, blankets, candles, or any other elements that inspire a sense of calm and relaxation.
4. **Focus on your breath**: One of the simplest meditation techniques is to focus on your breath. Inhale deeply, feeling the air fill your lungs, and exhale slowly, noticing the sensation of the breath leaving your body.
5. **Practice mindfulness throughout the day**: Cultivate mindfulness by directing your focus to the present moment. When engaged in any activity, notice the different sensory experiences, emotions, and thoughts arising without judgment.
6. **Be patient and compassionate**: It is natural for the mind to wander during meditation. When this happens, gently redirect your focus without judgment or frustration. Develop self-compassion and patience with your progress.

Conclusion

In a rapidly changing world full of distractions and stressors, it is all the more critical to prioritize our mental and emotional well-being. By cultivating mindfulness and integrating meditation practices into our daily lives, we can nurture inner peace, improve our relationships with ourselves and others, and enhance our overall quality of life. Take the time to unplug and nurture your inner world, even amidst the chaos of the external world.

6. Nurturing Meaningful Connections: Embracing Offline Conversations

Redefining Real Conversation in a Digital World

In the digital era we live in today, devices have become an integral part of our daily lives. Whether it's work, staying in touch with family and friends, or catching up with the news, we depend on the internet to keep us connected 24/7. While technology is an essential tool for keeping us engaged, it has also transformed the way we communicate with each other. The constant distractions caused by notifications, buzzing and beeping often lead to shallow connections and make us forget the importance of real, meaningful conversations.

In this chapter, we will explore why embracing offline conversations is vital for our mental health and relationships, and how we can start nurturing meaningful connections without the need for a screen.

The Power of Face-to-Face Interaction

Face-to-face conversations have a unique power to foster human connections. They allow us to see and feel the emotions of the people we're communicating with – whether it's a smile or a tear, a nod or a frown – and respond accordingly. These non-verbal cues enable us to build trust, understanding, and empathy, ultimately leading to deeper and more meaningful relationships.

Moreover, engaging in offline interactions encourages us to become better listeners, with the undivided attention we pay to the person in front of us. Taking the time to truly listen to someone's thoughts, experiences, and emotions allows for a valuable exchange of ideas and understanding.

Disconnecting to Reconnect

In order to nurture more significant offline connections, we need first to unplug from our devices and immerse ourselves in the physical world around us. Begin by designating specific times in your day when you set aside your devices and engage in face-to-face communication with those around you. This could mean sharing a meal, going for a walk or simply sitting down for a conversation. The idea is to make a conscious effort to be present and fully attentive during these moments.

Give meaningful conversations the time and space they deserve by:

- Turning off notifications: Silence your phone or put it on the quiet mode to minimize distractions during conversations.
- Designating device-free zones: Designate areas in your home or office as device-free zones where you can disconnect and engage in meaningful conversations with others.
- Scheduling regular offline time: Make it a habit to set aside regular offline time to engage with friends, family, and loved ones.

- Practising active listening: Make a conscious effort to listen actively to the person you're speaking with, acknowledging their thoughts and feelings.

Tips for Engaging in Offline Conversations

To reconnect with the art of meaningful conversation, consider the following steps:

1. **Share stories and personal experiences**: Dive deeper than casual small talk and share your thoughts, beliefs, and emotions authentically – this creates connections that last.
2. **Ask open-ended questions**: Avoid questions that will result in a simple 'yes' or 'no' answer. Instead, ask questions that encourage in-depth discussions and allow the other person to express their opinions.
3. **Show empathy**: Put yourself in the other person's shoes and genuinely try to understand their emotions, thoughts, and perspective. Give them the gift of your presence and undivided attention.
4. **Embrace silence**: It is natural for moments of silence to occur during a conversation. Instead of feeling compelled to fill the silence, embrace and appreciate it as a chance to process your thoughts and emotions.
5. **Avoid interrupting**: Become a more mindful listener by trying to avoid interrupting others, even if it's with well-intentioned advice or input. Give the other person the freedom to express themselves fully.

Foster Deeper Communication with Loved Ones

As you take steps to cultivate meaningful offline conversations, consider bringing that practice to your closest relationships – with your family, your partner, and your dearest friends. It's important to make deliberate and consistent efforts to engage in quality, face-to-face time with those we care about the most.

Try activities that encourage healthy communication and bonding, such as:

- Regular family dinners with a no-device rule
- Participating in hobbies or interests together
- Going on vacations or weekend getaways
- Collaborating on personal projects or goals

By embracing offline conversations and being mindful of our communication practices, we can create more meaningful connections and foster deeper relationships with the people around us, away from the distractions of our digital world. Remember, it's not just about disconnecting from our devices; it's about reconnecting with the people we hold dear and experiencing the beauty of each moment spent together.

Why Offline Conversations Matter

In a world that is increasingly dominated by digital communication, it's vital to remember the importance of offline conversations in forming and nurturing the connections that truly matter. Despite the convenience and widespread use of digital communication methods, they lack one key ingredient for cultivating strong relationships - presence. And presence is not just about being physically with someone, it goes beyond that, it is the experience of sharing moments, opening up and feeling a real connection. This chapter offers insight on how and why embracing offline conversations can bring profound value to your personal and professional life.

The Benefits of Offline Conversations

1. **Increased Empathy and Emotional Connection**: While online communication may seem efficient, it can often lead to a dearth of emotional connection. In-person conversations foster understanding and empathy; through non-verbal cues and emotional nuances, messages are communicated on a deeper level.
2. **Reduced Miscommunications**: In written or online communication, messages can often be misunderstood or misconstrued, as facial expressions and vocal inflections are absent. Offline conversations reduce the likelihood of such miscommunication, allowing you to convey your thoughts more effectively.
3. **Bond Building**: Sharing experiences, thoughts, and emotions in person is a powerful way to build strong bonds with friends, family, and colleagues. These shared experiences are the basis of deeply rooted attachment and trust, vital for healthy relationships.
4. **Personal Growth**: Conversations that happen offline often lead to personal growth and increased self-awareness. Engaging in thoughtful or challenging discussions can expand your perspectives, and deepen your understanding of the world and the people around you.
5. **Greater Communication Confidence**: The practice of engaging in face-to-face communication can lead to increased self-confidence, as you become more comfortable expressing yourself and navigating social situations. This can, in turn, lead to personal and professional success.

How to Foster Offline Conversations

1. **Make Time for Face-to-Face Interactions**: It's essential to prioritize in-person moments, even if it means going out of your way at times. Schedule

regular meetups, phone calls, or video calls with close friends and family members, allowing you to maintain and nurture your relationships.

2. **Set Technology Boundaries**: Embracing offline conversations means setting boundaries with your digital devices. Establish zones in your home where smartphones and other electronics are off-limits, such as the dining table, to encourage engaging conversation during meals.

3. **Be Present and Mindful**: When engaging in face-to-face communication, avoid distractions. Make a conscious effort to give the person you're speaking with your full attention, making eye contact and actively listening to what they have to say. Practicing mindfulness during conversations can help you better understand and connect with others.

4. **Embrace Vulnerability**: Allow yourself to be open, honest, and vulnerable during offline conversations. By revealing your thoughts, opinions, and emotions, you invite others to do the same, leading to more meaningful and emotionally connected conversations.

5. **Cultivate Empathy**: As you engage in face-to-face communication, make an effort to understand and empathize with others' perspectives, needs, and emotions. By displaying empathy, you not only strengthen your relationships, but also foster safe spaces for exploration and growth.

Taking it Further

In a world filled with digital distractions and shallow conversations, seeking out and embracing offline connections is essential for well-being and personal growth. The simple act of prioritizing face-to-face conversations with the people in your life can make a profound impact on your relationships and overall happiness. In addition, consider expanding your social network through various offline activities, such as joining clubs, attending workshops, or taking up group hobbies.

Don't undervalue the power of offline conversations in fostering empathy, strengthening bonds, and enriching your life. It's time to put down our devices and engage with the people and world around us. After all, as humans, our ability to connect deeply with one another is one of our most valuable assets.

Building Deeper Bonds through Face-to-Face Interactions

In today's fast-paced digital world, it can be all too easy to opt for the convenience of online communication over face-to-face conversations. While there's no denying the advantages that come with instant messaging and social media, it's crucial to remember the immense value of sitting down and connecting with someone in person. When we prioritize and engage in meaningful offline conversations, we're able to build stronger and more fulfilling relationships – a vital aspect of mindful living.

The Power of Face-to-Face Conversation

As humans, we're inherently social beings. We thrive on interaction and connection, and some of the most profound experiences in our lives are shared moments with others. While social media and other online platforms can facilitate these connections on a basic level, it's important to recognize that they cannot replace the unique romance, warmth and authenticity of face-to-face conversations. Here, we explore some of the crucial reasons why embracing offline conversations can be profoundly rewarding:

1. Enhanced Empathy and Emotional Connectivity: Sharing a physical space with another person allows us to communicate not just through words, but also through eye contact, body language, and facial expressions. These nonverbal cues provide valuable insights into the emotions and thoughts of others, fostering deeper empathy, understanding, and emotional bonding.

2. Improved Listening Skills: In a digital conversation, it's all too easy to multitask or become distracted, leading to shallow engagement and poorer communication skills. Face-to-face conversations, on the other hand, demand our full attention and offer the opportunity to practice active listening – an invaluable skill for all areas of life.

3. Context and Clarity: Text-based communication can be limiting, as important nuances are often lost amid the flatness of typed messages. Misunderstandings can easily arise, leading to hurt feelings or unnecessary conflicts. By contrast, the richness of face-to-face communication allows for greater clarity and understanding as we're able to observe and respond to verbal and nonverbal cues.

4. Building Trust and Authenticity: Online interactions, with their emphasis on carefully-managed self-presentation, can encourage superficiality and inauthenticity. Offline conversations, in contrast, provide a more accurate representation of who we are, allowing others to get to know the 'real' us. This helps to solidify trust and deepen bonds with our loved ones.

Tips for Cultivating Meaningful Offline Conversations

Now that we've explored the many benefits of engaging in face-to-face conversations, let's dive into some actionable tips for nurturing these connections:

1. Prioritize In-Person Meetups: In order to nurture deeper and more satisfying relationships, it's essential that we actively choose to make face-to-face interactions a priority in our lives. Consciously plan regular in-person meetups with friends, family, and colleagues by setting aside time for meals, outings, or simple walks.

2. Be Present and Mindful: When engaging in conversation, be fully present and attentive to the person you're talking to. Make a conscious effort to listen actively, maintaining eye contact, and using open body language to signal your engagement.

3. Turn Off Devices: One of the most effective ways to foster genuine connection with others is to eliminate potential distractions. When meeting with someone, make a deliberate effort to silence or even switch off your devices. This demonstrates respect and prioritizes the conversation at hand.

4. Ask Open-Ended Questions: Encourage deeper conversations by asking questions that invite elaboration and discussion. By probing further into a topic or sharing your own experiences, you can invite genuine insight, understanding, and empathy.

5. Embrace Vulnerability: Be willing to share your authentic thoughts, feelings, and experiences, even if doing so makes you feel vulnerable. This openness can facilitate real connection and understanding, helping to foster more intimate and trusting relationships.

In conclusion, offline conversations form an integral component of meaningful relationships and can significantly enhance our emotional well-being. By recognizing the importance of face-to-face interaction and actively cultivating these connections, we can take an important step toward mindful living.

Embracing Offline Conversations: Reclaiming the Lost Art of Connecting

While social media platforms and electronic devices promise us endless connections, are we still genuinely connecting with others? In an ever-connected digital world, our reliance on screens and online platforms has created a chasm in real-life conversations, leaving friendships, relationships, and family connections in jeopardy.

Much has been discussed about the detrimental effects of screen time, but what about the lost opportunities to connect with others, share new experiences, or create unforgettable memories together? In this chapter, we'll explore why reclaiming the lost art of face-to-face conversations is crucial, and how you can nurture meaningful connections offline.

The Power of Genuine Interaction

Face-to-face conversations are essential for fostering genuine human connections. Human presence and eye contact deepen mutual understanding, and physical touch, such as hugs or a pat on the back, provide hormonal benefits that boost our overall well-being. Genuine interaction creates a shared experience that both parties can build upon, benefit from, and cherish.

Nothing can replace the emotional intensity achieved through real-life connections. Social cues, such as body language and tone of voice, simply cannot be conveyed in the same way through digital communication. These nuances are fundamental to building trust, empathy, and companionship, and they need to be cultivated through in-person engagements.

Making Time for Offline Conversations

As our attention span grows shorter and we become disenchanted with our screens, we can make an active decision to shift our focus to the offline world. Here are a few ways to make space for enriching conversations:

1. **Set boundaries for digital use**: Establish designated periods of abstinence from electronics, such as an hour before bedtime or a day during the weekend, and encourage family members to do the same. Use this time to strike up a conversation, enjoy a meal together, or engage in fulfilling activities.
2. **Create safe spaces for discussion**: Conversations and discussions deserve a level of importance, meaning they require an undisturbed environment—free from digital interruptions or distractions. Establish a common area in your home, like a living room or patio, where everyone can gather for an exchange of thoughts and ideas.
3. **Declare non-screen zones**: Libraries, parks, and outdoor venues are perfect spaces for conversation, devoid of the distractions brought on by screens. Use these sanctuaries to engage with friends, family, or even strangers, allowing you to expand your social network.
4. **Promote open-ended conversations**: Encourage open-ended discussions by asking meaningful

questions that delve deeper into personal experiences, values, and aspirations. Resist steering the conversation towards gossip or small talk exclusively. Instead, focus on profound discussions that create long-lasting connections.

5. **Make time for one-on-one meetups**: Instead of group gatherings, opt for individual interactions where possible. Personal meetings with friends, family, or colleagues provide an intimate setting for bonding, understanding, and appreciation not often found in group dynamics.

6. **Listen actively**: Embrace your role as an active listener, and be present for the person initiating the conversation. Validate their feelings, absorb their story, and show empathy—these actions will go a long way in building a strong connection.

Building a Community Offline

Engaging in offline conversations is essential for establishing communities and support networks. Face-to-face interactions create a sense of unity, which is crucial for overall well-being, whereas online interactions often foster comparison, competition, and only reveal a limited scope of a person's life.

By connecting with people offline, we develop genuine relationships that reflect all facets of our personality, not only the highlights we select for our online presence. As we embrace the real world, we realize that nurturing meaningful connections is the antidote to the alienation and despair derived from our digital existence.

Remember, the key to engaging offline conversations is intentionality. Make time for in-person interactions, and incorporate meaningful exchange into your daily life. By doing so, you'll experience the immeasurable rewards of genuine connections—improved mental health and emotional well-being, as well as a sense of belonging and appreciation.

It's time to unplug and nurture our connections in the here and now, so let's embrace the lost art of offline conversations and rediscover the joy of human connection.

Face-to-Face Interactions: The Power of Human Connection

In our ever-connected digital world, one might argue that communication has become easier than ever. We can stay in touch with friends and loved ones living miles away with just a few taps and swipes, send messages instantaneously, and even communicate with people from different cultures without knowing their language, thanks to translation tools.

While it's true that the digital age has brought countless opportunities for connection, it has also caused many of us to forget the value of face-to-face interaction. Indeed, the convenience of digital communication often leads us to ignore the person sitting right in front of us. In this chapter, we will explore the significance of engaging in offline conversations and rediscovering the power of human connection.

The Science behind Face-to-Face Communication

There are multiple reasons why engaging in face-to-face conversation holds greater significance than its digital counterparts. For starters, these interactions engage all our senses—sight, sound, touch—allowing for a more nuanced and multidimensional understanding of the messages being conveyed. We also better understand the context in which it's being relayed, resulting in richer communication experiences.

Recent studies have even shown that face-to-face communication fosters empathy and trust between individuals in ways that chatting online simply cannot replicate. This is partly due to the formation of nonverbal cues such as facial expressions, gestures, tone of voice, and eye contact that are essential in creating a sense of connection and understanding between people.

The hormone oxytocin, often referred to as the "love hormone," is also known to be released during moments of physical touch and social bonding, strengthening our bonds and allowing us to experience a greater sense of belonging. In other words, physical presence is not only essential for effective communication but also plays a vital role in our emotional well-being.

Creating Opportunities for Offline Conversations

In order to foster more face-to-face interactions or offline conversations, you should first recognize the importance of "unplugging" and giving your full attention to the people around you. Resisting the urge to check your phone every few minutes or answer messages during social gatherings is key, as these habits prevent you from being fully present in the moment.

Here are some steps you can take towards embracing offline conversations:

1. **Set boundaries with technology**: Determine specific times when you will allow yourself to engage with

digital devices, and avoid using them during other times, especially when you are with others. Create "device-free" zones in your home, such as bedrooms or the dining table, and ensure that all members of your household respect these boundaries.
2. **Plan regular face-to-face interactions**: Make an effort to schedule regular in-person meetings with friends, family, or colleagues. This can include weekly coffee dates, family dinners, or even just casual walks in the park.
3. **Join clubs and organizations**: Engage in social activities like book clubs, sports teams, or volunteer work that encourage interaction with others. These activities provide numerous occasions for offline conversations and promote the development of social connections.
4. **Practice active listening**: When speaking with someone face-to-face, focus on giving them your full attention and truly hearing what they have to say. Nod your head, maintain eye contact, and refrain from interrupting or formulating your response while they are still talking.
5. **Embrace vulnerability**: To foster deeper connections, be willing to share your thoughts and feelings openly and honestly with others. Doing so requires trust, and in turn, helps to build that trust.

By prioritizing face-to-face interactions, you facilitate the growth of genuine connections with the people in your life, making your relationships more meaningful, and ultimately, enhancing your overall well-being.

The Benefits of Embracing Offline Conversations

Integrating more offline conversations into your daily life offers numerous advantages beyond improving your communication skills. These benefits include:

- Strengthening social and emotional bonds
- Reducing stress and anxiety
- Boosting self-esteem and confidence
- Enhancing the ability to empathize and understand others
- Developing healthy communication habits

Moreover, it's important to remember that technology should serve as a tool to enhance our lives, not replace the basic human need for connection and interaction. When used mindfully, digital communication can act as a valuable supplement to our face-to-face relationships. By striking the right balance, we can continue to benefit from the digital age while not losing touch with the importance of human connection.

7. Digital Detox Challenges and Strategies: A Step-by-Step Guide

Challenge 1: The Social Media Detox

Strategy

Step 1: Assess your social media usage

Before you start your digital detox, it's essential to evaluate your relationship with social media. This will help you understand how much time you spend on it daily and identify which apps you need to detox from.

- Track your screen time
- Make a list of social media apps used
- Rank apps according to time spent on each daily

Step 2: Set realistic goals

It's crucial to set achievable goals to keep yourself on track throughout the detox process.

- Define a specific timeframe (e.g., a week, a month)
- Establish checkpoints to track your progress (e.g., check your screen time at the end of each day)

Step 3: Turn off notifications

To reduce distractions and the urge to continuously check your phone, turn off all social media notifications on your devices.

- Go to your device settings and disable notifications for each app listed in step 1.

Step 4: Create alternative activities

In order to fill the void caused by the lack of social media, plan alternative activities that promote mindfulness and well-being.

- Physical: exercise, walk, yoga
- Cognitive: read, write, solve puzzles
- Social: meet friends, join community events, volunteer
- Emotional: practice meditation, deep breathing exercises, awareness reflection

Step 5: Evaluation

Evaluate your progress periodically to ensure you stay on track with your goals.

- Review your screen time at each checkpoint
- Assess how well you are coping without social media
- Reflect on any challenges faced and how you overcame them

Step 6: Reintroduction

Once your detox has reached its conclusion, reintroduce social media gradually and mindfully.

- Start with one app at a time
- Set usage limits or use a timer to avoid overindulgence
- Continue practicing alternative activities to maintain a healthy balance

Challenge 2: Reducing Screen Time Before Bed

Strategy

Step 1: Acknowledge the importance of sleep

Realize the value of a good night's sleep and how screens can interfere with your ability to relax and fall asleep.

- Research about the blue light emitted by screens and its effect on sleep
- Reflect on how your pre-bedtime screen habits affect your sleep quality

Step 2: Set a digital curfew

Designate a specific hour in the evening as your nightly "tech-free" time.

- Choose a time that is realistic, yet challenging (e.g. one hour before bed)
- Ensure appropriate alarms or reminders are set to help you maintain consistency

Step 3: Create a bedtime routine

Establishing a calming bedtime routine promotes relaxation and can help signal to your body that it's time to sleep.

- Incorporate relaxing activities such as reading, light stretching, or deep breathing exercises
- Consider using essential oils, herbal teas, or calming sounds to create a soothing atmosphere

Step 4: Designate a charging station away from your bed

Charge your phone or digital devices in a separate room or designate a specific area away from your bed to reduce any temptation to use them.

- Establish a "no devices in bed" rule to maintain a sleep-friendly environment
- Consider investing in an alarm clock instead of using your phone to reduce dependency and morning screen time

Step 5: Reflect and adjust

As with any new habit, it's crucial to monitor your progress, adjust goals as needed, and maintain determination.

- Reflect on the quality of your sleep and overall well-being
- Identify areas of improvement or where further changes are needed

- Continue incorporating strategies until they become habitual and effortless

Challenge 3: Mindful Email Management

Strategy

Step 1: Establish designated email times

Limit your email checking to specific times throughout the day to avoid constant distractions.

- Set specific times for checking and responding to emails (e.g. mid-morning, after lunch, and end of the day)
- Block out these designated times on your calendar or to-do list

Step 2: Set expectations

Communicate to colleagues, friends, or clients about your email management strategy to avoid unnecessary stress or misunderstandings.

- Include a brief note in your email signature or within an autoresponder message explaining your response strategy
- Encourage alternative communication methods for urgent matters (e.g. phone calls or instant messaging)

Step 3: Organize and prioritize

Organize your inbox using folders and filters, enabling you to process emails more efficiently and effectively.

- Create folders or categories to sort emails depending on their importance or urgency
- Use filters and rules to automate the sorting process

Step 4: Maintain a clean inbox

Regularly clean and declutter your inbox to avoid feeling overwhelmed by your email correspondence.

- Develop daily or weekly habits of archiving, deleting or forwarding emails that no longer require your attention
- Unsubscribe from email newsletters or promotions that are no longer valuable or relevant

Step 5: Review and refine

Continuously assess and adapt your email management strategy based on your personal experience and requirements.

- Reflect on how well the strategy is working and whether any additional changes are necessary
- Remain open to modifications and adjustments in response to evolving work or personal circumstances

Facing the Digital Detox Hurdles: Taking One Step at a Time

Embarking on a digital detox journey isn't without its challenges, but facing them head-on and adopting mindful strategies can pave the way for successful, long-lasting changes in your digital lifestyle. The following step-by-step guide will help you navigate these challenges and offer support for your digital detox.

1. Identifying Triggers and Habits

The first step in any detox process is identifying the problem areas, recognizing precisely which digital habits bother you, and being aware of when and why you indulge in them. Pay attention to the triggers that prompt excessive digital usage, such as:

- Feeling stressed or anxious
- Procrastinating on important tasks
- Trying to escape real-life problems
- Fear of missing out on social events and news

2. Setting Clear Goals

To ensure success in your digital detox, set clear, achievable goals that you can work toward. These might include reducing screen-time hours, spending digital time more mindfully, reconnecting with loved ones, or simply enhancing mental well-being. Be realistic yet ambitious with your objectives, challenging yourself to make lasting changes.

3. Planning in Advance

Like embarking on a diet, digital detox requires thorough planning to prevent temptation later on—after all, you're likely to encounter tempting digital distractions even when your intention is to stay unplugged. Anticipate these scenarios and devise your strategies to handle them:

- Inform friends, family, and work colleagues in advance about your plan to detox. They can offer essential emotional support and understanding.
- Prepare alternative activities to fill the time that you'd usually spend connected. Try journaling, reading, sports, or creative pursuits.

- Set boundaries, such as designated times and locations for digital use, to avoid mindless scrolling and ensure more mindful engagement with technology.

4. Embrace New Mindsets and Strategies

Develop a well-rounded, mindful approach to digital interaction by incorporating these helpful tactics:

- Prioritize the quality of your digital engagement over quantity: Focus your online presence on meaningful conversations, connections, and resources instead of being everywhere at once.
- Practice gratitude and mindfulness when using digital devices. Take the time to fully appreciate the convenience, entertainment, and personal connections they offer—this can prevent a sense of digital burnout.
- No-device zones: Designate specific areas and times in your home and daily routine where digital devices are off-limits.

5. Building New Connections

One of the essential aspects of your digital detox journey is creating new connections or strengthening existing ones. Fill the void left by digital distractions with enriching face-to-face interactions, group activities, and community involvement.

- Attempt new hobbies or group sports that encourage real-life socializing.
- Plan regular gatherings with friends and loved ones that promote conversation, laughter, and joy.

- Volunteer for community-related causes to experience a sense of accomplishment, purpose, and camaraderie.

6. Monitoring Progress and Staying Accountable

Evaluate your progress regularly, track the improvements you make, and keep yourself accountable. Make adjustments when necessary and remember that success isn't just about following a strict plan. It's about adapting to and growing through the challenges that arise:

- Keep a journal to record the changes, challenges, and milestones you encounter throughout your digital detox journey.
- Share your progress with a designated detox buddy, who can offer valuable advice, support, and encouragement.
- Help others with their digital detox, acting as a mentor and support for friends, family members, or anyone looking to embark on a mindful technology journey.

7. Celebrating Successes and Lessons Learned

Finally, don't forget to take pride in your achievements and find joy in the lessons learned during your digital detox. Whether you've cut down on screen time, fostered closer connections, or simply become more mindful about your digital usage, these steps go a long way in improving the balance between technology and real-life experiences. No matter how small or significant, every positive change matters, and with dedication and perseverance, these changes can have a lasting impact on your well-being.

By following this step-by-step guide to digital detox challenges and strategies, you'll be well on your way to enjoying a more mindful, balanced, and fulfilling life—one that's less dominated by digital distractions and more enriched with authentic connections and experiences.

Challenge 3: Nurture Mindful Communication and Relationships

The world we live in is so interconnected that the line between the virtual and the real world has become increasingly blurred. Social media and instant messaging have completely revolutionized the way we communicate with each other. However, the costs of such convenience cannot be ignored as we often find ourselves getting lost in endless conversations on our screens and losing touch with those around us. This challenge involves adopting mindful communication practices and deepening our real-life connections.

Step 1: Make an inventory of digital communications

Begin by taking a closer look at how you communicate with others through digital means. Make an inventory of all communication platforms that you use, such as social media, emails, instant messaging, and forums. Make notes of the type of interactions that you have on each platform, whether it is work-related, friendships, or casual networking. Observe the frequency and time of day when you engage in digital communication the most.

Step 2: Set limits and boundaries for digital communication

Now that you have a clearer understanding of your digital communication habits, it's time to establish some boundaries. Establish time limits for each platform and stick to them. Reduce unnecessary browsing, scrolling, and posting on social networks, and focus only on meaningful interactions. Turn off notifications for minor events and filter your social media feeds so you only receive updates from close friends and family.

Step 3: Cultivate mindful communication

As you work to reduce the frequency and duration of digital communication, it's important to also improve the quality of the interactions you have online. Focus on engaging in deep conversations and avoid digital small talk. Listen closely to what others are saying and take time to craft meaningful responses. When interacting through text, be aware of your tone and how it may be conveyed through your written words. Always aim to be patient and respectful in your digital interactions.

Step 4: Develop digital-free conversations

Once you have limited your digital interactions, focus on establishing deep and meaningful connections in real life. When talking with others, make sure to put your phone on silent or keep it out of sight. Be fully present and attuned to the moment and the person you are talking to. Encourage others to do the same, sparking digital-free conversations where everyone feels valued and heard.

Step 5: Nurture offline relationships

Finally, make your offline relationships a top priority. Plan face-to-face meetings with friends and family, rekindle old friendships, and explore new hobbies that involve interacting with others. These activities will strengthen your interpersonal connections and remind you of the benefits of forging deeper relationships in real life.

Step 6: Reflect on your journey

While on your journey toward mindful communication and deepening your relationships, make sure to regularly reflect on your progress. Observe the changes in your state of mind, your relationships, and how you feel overall. Note down your observations in a journal or a digital document, and keep refining and adjusting your communication habits based on your experiences and growth.

By focusing on cultivating mindful communication and nurturing meaningful relationships offline, you will find yourself more connected and engaged in the real world. As you move through these steps, remember that the goal is not to shun digital communication altogether but to integrate it sensibly and thoughtfully into your life.

Challenge 1: Start with a Digital Detox Audit

Before diving into your digital detox journey, it is important to assess your current state of digital consumption. A digital detox audit helps you identify your patterns, habits, and areas that may need improvement or scaling back.

Step 1.1: Track Your Screen Time

Monitor your screen time for an entire week, including work and personal time. Most smartphones and tablets have built-in screen time tracking features. You can also install apps like *RescueTime* or *Freedom* on your devices to track the time you spend online and on specific apps.

Step 1.2: Analyze Your Patterns

After a week, review the data and identify areas where you spend the most time. Are you spending a lot of time on social media? Watching videos? Gaming? Identify the top three applications or services that consume most of your screen time.

Step 1.3: Determine Your Digital Priorities

Consider which digital activities are essential to your well-being, personal growth, and professional success. Determine which digital activities can be reduced or eliminated entirely.

Challenge 2: Set Digital Boundaries

Once you have a clear understanding of your current digital consumption, it's time to set boundaries to establish a healthy balance between online and offline activities.

Step 2.1: Set Daily Screen Time Limits

Establish a daily screen time limit for non-essential activities (like social media, videos, or games). Apps like *Forest* or *AppDetox* can help you enforce these limits by blocking certain applications after your daily limit has been reached.

Step 2.2: Schedule Digital-Free Time

Carve out specific periods during the day or week when you completely unplug from digital devices. This could mean scheduling a short evening walk without your phone, dedicating a full day to exploring nature, or setting aside specific hours every day when devices are off-limits.

Step 2.3: Limit Notifications

Reduce distractions by disabling unnecessary notifications on your devices. Keep only the essential notifications, such as important email or work-related chat messages, active.

Challenge 3: Cultivate Mindful Tech Use

Mindfulness can help you become more aware of your digital habits and equip you to make better decisions about how and when to engage with technology.

Step 3.1: Develop a "Mindful Check-In" Routine

Before unlocking your phone or opening your laptop, take a moment to ask yourself: "Why am I doing this? Is it necessary, or am I just seeking distraction?" Pause and evaluate if engaging with that particular device is the best use of your time in that moment.

Step 3.2: Practice Single-Tasking

Give your full attention to one task at a time, rather than multitasking. This can lead to greater productivity and help reduce stress.

Step 3.3: Create a Mindful Digital Environment

Declutter your digital space by deleting unused apps or accounts and turning off unnecessary devices. Create a clean and organized digital environment that promotes focus and reduces distractions.

Challenge 4: Foster Meaningful Offline Connections

Cultivate meaningful connections and experiences outside of the digital realm to strengthen your relationships and enrich your life.

Step 4.1: Host Tech-Free Social Gatherings

Organize events where everyone commits to unplugging and engaging in activities like board games, book clubs, hiking, or art projects.

Step 4.2: Encourage Face-to-Face Communication

When possible, opt for in-person conversations over digital communication. Discuss the idea of creating "phone-free zones" or "phone stacking" with friends and family, where everyone puts their devices away to focus solely on engaging with one another.

Step 4.3: Participate in Offline Hobbies and Interests

Explore new hobbies or restart interest in existing ones that do not involve digital devices. This can be anything from painting, gardening, or playing a musical instrument.

Challenge 5: Develop a Supportive System

Effectively managing a digital detox requires building a strong support system that encourages you to maintain healthy digital habits long-term.

Step 5.1: Share your Goals

Discuss your digital detox intentions with friends, family, and colleagues, and ask for their support in helping you establish new habits. The more people know about your plans, the more accountable you will feel.

Step 5.2: Connect with Like-Minded Individuals

Join groups or forums online where people share their experiences with digital detoxes, discussing tips, and offering support.

Remember that embarking on a digital detox is a personal journey, and there's no "one size fits all" approach. Be patient with yourself and take the time to adjust your habits to achieve a healthier balance between your digital and offline activities.

Challenge 1: Screen-Free Morning Routine

Strategy: Start your day without checking your phone or turning on your computer. Instead, engage in a relaxing and mindful morning routine, such as meditation, yoga, reading or even going for a walk. By doing so, you will set a positive tone for the day, cultivate a sense of inner peace, and become more aware of how much time you would habitually spend on screens in the morning.

1. Prepare for your screen-free morning the night before: Set an intention to avoid all digital devices upon waking up, place your phone in another room, and lay out some items to support your morning routine, such as a book, journal, or yoga mat.
2. Develop a consistent wake-up time: It will be easier to maintain a screen-free morning routine if you develop a consistent sleep schedule, waking up at the same time each day.
3. Engage in a mindful activity: Pick an activity that calms your mind and focuses your attention inward, such as meditation, deep breathing exercises, or gentle stretching.
4. Make a nourishing breakfast: Take the time to make a healthy breakfast, and enjoy this meal without any screens in front of you. Consider sitting at a table, looking out a window, or even having breakfast outside to connect with the natural world.
5. Engage in an enjoyable non-screen activity: After breakfast, fill your morning with activities that you enjoy and that don't require electronic devices. This could include reading, writing in a journal, going for a walk, or spending time with your family or pets.

Challenge 2: Mindful Commute

Strategy: Use your commuting time to be present, observe your surroundings, and practice deep breathing or meditation techniques to create a serene space within yourself, rather than using electronic devices to distract yourself from the experience of commuting.

1. Leave your phone in your bag or pocket: To resist the temptation to use digital devices during your commute, keep your phone out of sight and try to forget about it.
2. Engage your senses: Take notice of the sights, sounds, and smells around you while commuting, whether it be the changing landscape, people's faces, or the aroma of coffee stands. This heightened awareness can bring you into the present moment.
3. Deep breathing: When you find your mind wandering or stress levels rising, engage in deep breathing exercises to calm your body and mind.
4. Find pockets of quiet: If you use public transportation, try to find seats or areas that are quieter, where you can avoid being bombarded with digital screens, advertisements and people talking on their phones.
5. Consider alternative transportation: Walking or cycling to work can be a great way to limit your screen time, while also enjoying the physical and mental health benefits of physical activity.

Challenge 3: Device-Free Meals

Strategy: Create a healthy relationship with food by eliminating screen distractions during your meals. This will help you savor the flavors and textures of your food, encourage healthy digestion, and foster more connected conversations with the people around you.

1. Make a commitment: Establish a clear intention to keep devices away from meals and communicate this intention to those who share meals with you.

2. Create device-free zones: Designate the dining table as a device-free zone, where phones, tablets, and laptops are strictly off-limits.
3. Build connection: Use mealtime to foster face-to-face conversation, share stories from your day, and strengthen your relationships with family members or friends.
4. Practice mindful eating: Focus on the flavors, textures, and aromas of your food, as well as the feeling of fullness as you eat. This will help you consume your meal at a slower pace, preventing overeating.
5. Cultivate gratitude: Before you begin your meal, take a moment to express gratitude for the food, as well as the people who helped bring it to your table.

Challenge 4: Purposeful Social Media Usage

Strategy: Treat social media as a tool, rather than a pastime, by setting intentions for your usage and establishing boundaries that prevent it from consuming too much of your time and attention.

1. Define your intentions: Be clear about why you use social media and how it adds value to your life. If it doesn't serve a specific purpose, reconsider your engagement with it.
2. Set time limits: Allocate a specific amount of time each day for social media use, and stick to this limit. Using an app or timer can help you track your usage and keep you accountable.

3. Remove unnecessary apps: Delete social media apps
   that don't align with your intentions, or those that
   seem to consume an excessive amount of your time.
4. Curate your feed: Unfollow or mute accounts that
   don't bring value to your life, and focus on content that
   aligns with your values, goals, and interests.
5. Engage mindfully: When using social media, be
   present and interact with others in a meaningful way,
   rather than mindlessly scrolling or consuming content.

Challenge 5: Screen-Free Evening Wind-Down

Strategy: Design a calming and relaxing evening routine
that helps you transition from the day's activities and
promotes restful sleep, while also reducing your exposure to
screens and their accompanying blue light emissions.

1. Set a screen curfew: Establish a specific time in the
   evening when all digital devices are turned off and put
   away, ideally 1-2 hours before your bedtime.
2. Create a cozy atmosphere: Prepare a relaxing
   environment in your home that encourages
   restfulness, such as dimming the lights, lighting
   candles, or playing soft music.
3. Engage in a calming activity: Participate in an
   engaging and low-stress activity that helps you
   unwind, such as reading a book, taking a bath, or
   practicing gentle stretches or yoga.
4. Reflect on your day: Spend some time reflecting on
   your day, either through journaling or a mental review,
   allowing you to process your thoughts and emotions
   before sleep.

5. Sleep hygiene: Encourage restful sleep by making
    your bedroom a sanctuary, with a comfortable bed,
    dark curtains or shades, and a cool temperature.

By embracing these digital detox challenges and strategies,
you will harness the power of mindfulness, improve your
physical and mental health, and develop a greater
appreciation for the present moment. Fostering a healthy
balance with technology will enhance your overall well-being
and the quality of your relationships with others, allowing you
to rediscover the simple joys in life.

8. Incorporating Mindfulness into Daily Life: Practical Tips and Exercises

Daily Mindfulness Practices: Simple Techniques for a Balanced Life

In today's fast-paced, technology-driven world, it is more
important than ever to find moments of stillness and cultivate
mindfulness in our daily lives. Mindfulness is not just a
practice reserved for meditation cushions or yoga studios; it

is a constant, intentional choice we can make every day to live more authentically, compassionately, and peacefully.

The following practical tips and exercises will help you on your journey to integrate mindfulness into your daily life, so that you can reap its numerous benefits and promote a more balanced, grounded, and focused existence.

1. Morning Intention-Setting

Begin your day with a morning intention-setting practice. Before you reach for your phone or get out of bed, take a few deep breaths and tune into the present moment. Set a simple intention for your day, such as being more patient, staying present, or practicing gratitude. Visualize embodying this intention throughout the day and return to it as needed.

2. Mindful Breathing

Mindful breathing is a foundational practice for cultivating mindfulness. Throughout your day, take moments (even if it's just for a few breaths) to close your eyes and tune into the sensations of your breath. Notice the rise and fall of your chest or the sensation of air entering and leaving your nostrils.

This simple practice can have a significant impact on reducing stress and anxiety, as it brings you back to the present moment and increases focus.

3. Technology Breaks

With the prevalence of smartphones, we are constantly tethered to our digital lives. Set specific times for technology breaks throughout your day – times when you intentionally unplug from your devices and give yourself space from the digital world.

During these breaks, engage in grounding activities like taking a walk, journaling, or even just sitting and observing the world around you. This practice will help curb the incessant need to check our devices and promote a healthier balance between the digital and physical world.

4. Mindful Eating

Too often, our meals are consumed in front of screens or on-the-go. Take the opportunity to practice mindful eating during meals by removing distractions and focusing on the sensations, flavors, and textures of your food. Take time to chew, savor, and appreciate each bite as you nourish your body.

This practice can help improve digestion, eating habits, and your relationship with food by bringing awareness and intention to the act of eating.

5. Body Scan Meditation

A body scan meditation is a simple practice that cultivates awareness of the physical body and its sensations. You can incorporate this practice into your daily routine by setting aside 5-10 minutes to lie down or sit comfortably and mentally scan your body from head to toe.

Notice any areas of tension or discomfort, and imagine your breath flowing through these areas, releasing tension and promoting relaxation. This practice fosters a deeper connection to your body and allows you to recognize and release physical manifestations of stress more effectively.

6. Gratitude Journaling

Cultivating an attitude of gratitude is essential for a mindful life. One way to establish this practice is by keeping a daily gratitude journal. At the end of each day, write down three things for which you are grateful.

This simple exercise brings awareness to the abundance of blessings in your life and promotes positive thinking and contentment in the face of challenges or uncertainty.

7. Anchor Points

Create anchor points throughout your day – specific moments where you intentionally pause and check in with yourself. This can be as simple as taking a deep breath and grounding yourself before entering a meeting or starting a new task.

Use these anchor points to observe your current mental and emotional state, then choose appropriate mindful practices (e.g., deep breathing, reciting a mantra, or practicing loving-kindness meditation) to help you recalibrate if needed.

8. Mindful Communication

Practicing mindful communication involves active listening, thoughtfulness, and presence. Make a conscious effort to listen and respond thoughtfully to others, noticing any urges to interrupt or react emotionally. Cultivate a compassionate and understanding attitude, and strive to truly connect with others as you engage in conversation.

By incorporating these practical tips and exercises into your daily life, you will be on your way to cultivating a deeper sense of mindfulness, inner peace, and balance. Always remember that mindfulness is a lifelong practice, and every small moment of presence and intention can have a profound impact on your overall well-being and quality of life.

8.1 Developing a Mindful Morning Routine

An excellent way to begin incorporating mindfulness into your daily life is to create a mindful morning routine. This means you'll start your day with intention and purpose, giving yourself a solid foundation for the rest of the day. Here are some tips and exercises to help you develop a consistent and nourishing morning routine:

1. **Wake up mindfully**: As soon as you wake up, resist the immediate urge to reach for your phone or jump out of bed. Instead, take a few deep breaths and become aware of your body sensations, thoughts, and emotions. This short pause will allow you to fully wake up and connect with the present moment.
2. **Stretch and hydrate**: Begin your morning with a light stretch to awaken your body and increase your energy levels. Doing so helps to disperse any lingering grogginess and prepares your body for the day. Drinking a glass of water immediately after waking up can also help to rehydrate your body and promote a sense of alertness.
3. **Meditate**: Set aside 5 to 15 minutes for meditation, focusing on your breath or performing a body scan. Starting your day with meditation boosts your mental clarity and emotional balance, making it easier to navigate through the rest of the day with mindfulness.
4. **Morning pages**: Consider journaling for 10 to 20 minutes as part of your daily routine. This can be a free-flowing practice in which you write down

whatever comes to mind, getting your thoughts and emotions out of your head and onto paper. Not only is this an effective means of self-debriefing, but it can also spark new ideas and insights.

5. **Movement**: Incorporate physical movement, whether it's yoga, walking, running, or dancing. Exercise boosts mood and energy, along with offering countless physical benefits. As you move, focus on the sensations in your body and the connection between your body and the ground. This practice encourages mindfulness as you stay aware of your physical presence.

6. **Mindful eating**: Eat your breakfast slowly, paying attention to the taste, texture, and aroma of the food. Concentrate on the sensation of chewing and swallowing, savoring each bite. This practice not only enhances your enjoyment of the meal but also encourages improved digestion.

7. **Gratitude**: Note three things — small or big — that you're grateful for in your life. You may find it helpful to write these down in a journal or share them with a loved one. This positive reflection brings your focus to the present moment and primes your mind for positivity throughout the day.

8. **Set intentions**: Before diving into the day, set a clear intention or goal that you want to achieve. This could be anything from maintaining a present state of mind to accomplishing a specific task. Keeping this intention in mind helps to keep you grounded and maintain a sense of purpose throughout the day.

9. **Limit exposure to digital devices**: As you're performing these morning routines, avoid using your phone, tablet, or computer. This time is reserved for cultivating mindfulness and a connection with your body and surroundings. By staying away from digital

distractions, you'll also reduce the chances of the day's stressors seeping into your morning routines.

Remember: consistency is key

Creating a mindful morning routine can be challenging at first; it takes time and consistent practice to develop these new habits. The key is to be patient and gentle with yourself as you work through the process. With consistent effort and practice, these mindful morning rituals will become an essential and enjoyable aspect of your daily life.

8.2 Cultivating a Mindful Morning Routine

The first moments of your day are crucial to establish a mindful foundation and set a positive tone for each day. Taking control of your morning routine is key to beginning your day with calm, clarity, and focus. In this section, we explore various practical tips and exercises to help you pave the way for a more mindful and intentional day.

8.2.1 Start with Intention

Before you even open your eyes in the morning, take a moment to focus on your breath and set an intention for the day. It can be as simple as choosing an area in your life that you would like to pay attention to, or it can be a commitment to maintain a positive mindset. Setting an intention helps guide your day towards meaningful action and gives a sense of purpose.

8.2.2 Meditate

Developing a daily meditation practice is one of the most powerful tools in cultivating mindfulness. Ideally, commit to meditating for at least 10-15 minutes each morning. Find a quiet and comfortable space where you can sit in a relaxed position. Focus your attention on your breath, and gently bring your mind back whenever it wanders. Overtime, you'll notice an increased ability to remain present and observe your thoughts and emotions without judgment.

8.2.3 Practice Gratitude

Before you get out of bed, take a moment to consciously acknowledge three things you are grateful for. It could be as simple as appreciating the warm bed you're lying in, the presence of a loved one, or the opportunity to have a fresh start each day. Practicing gratitude encourages a positive perspective and helps you approach each day with an open heart.

8.2.4 Avoid Technology

Resist the urge to reach for your phone or laptop first thing in the morning. Checking emails, social media or the news can easily clutter your mind with unnecessary information and stressors. Instead, allow yourself to ground and center through mindful activities before engaging with the digital world.

8.2.5 Stretch and Move Mindfully

Begin your day by doing some gentle stretching or light physical activity, such as yoga, tai chi, or even a short walk outside. Bringing movement into your morning routine not only kickstarts your metabolism but also wakes up your body and brings awareness to your physical being.

8.2.6 Nourish Your Body

As you prepare your breakfast, focus on selecting healthy and nutritious options. Be present during the preparation and cooking process, noticing the smells, textures, and tastes of the ingredients. Enjoy your meal slowly and mindfully, considering how the food you choose to eat contributes to your health and well-being.

8.2.7 Create a Mindful Space

Designate an area in your home as your 'mindful space' – a place where you can sit, reflect, journal, or engage in activities that encourage mindfulness. Maintain its simplicity and cleanliness to make it a space you feel drawn to and can find peace in.

8.2.8 Establish a Consistent Routine

Consistency is key when integrating mindfulness into your daily life. Develop a morning routine that includes activities promoting mindfulness, and make it a non-negotiable part of your day. Over time, the routine will become second nature, allowing for a smooth transition into a more mindful lifestyle.

8.2.9 Cultivate Meaningful Connections

Take time in the morning to connect with yourself and your loved ones. Share your intentions for the day, practice active listening, or write a letter of appreciation. Building and maintaining meaningful connections can increase feelings of happiness and create a strong support system for your mindfulness journey.

8.2.10 Reflect on Your Progress

As you integrate mindfulness into your daily life, it's important to regularly reflect on your progress. Journaling may be particularly helpful here to track your experiences, insights, and challenges. This reflection time also allows you to make adjustments as needed to continually personalizing your daily routine.

Incorporating mindfulness into your daily life requires continuous effort and commitment, but taking these steps to cultivate a fruitful morning routine can make the transition easier. As you practice being present and attentive, you'll reap the rewards of a more fulfilling, balanced, and meaningful life.

8. Incorporating Mindfulness into Daily Life: Practical Tips and Exercises

Society today is driven by the continuous onslaught of information and distractions provided by our digital devices. This can make it difficult to stay present and often leads to increased feelings of stress and anxiety. Mindfulness is a practice that counteracts these common difficulties by promoting present moment awareness, emotional regulation, and mental wellbeing. In this section, we'll explore a range of practical tips and exercises that you can use to bring greater mindfulness into your daily life.

1. Start with a morning routine:

Begin your day with a focus on mindfulness by establishing a morning routine that incorporates activities to promote present-moment awareness. This can include:

- Meditation – Start your day with a 10-20 minute mindfulness meditation, focusing your attention on your breath, body sensations, or a mantra.

- Yoga – Yoga helps develop a greater mind-body connection and combines meditation, breathwork, and physical movement.
- Journaling – Dedicate a few moments each morning to writing down your thoughts, feelings, and intentions for the day. This practice can help you cultivate self-awareness and create a proactive approach to the day ahead.
- Gratitude – Begin your day with an attitude of gratitude, listing three things you are grateful for each morning. This simple practice heightens your awareness of the positive aspects of your life and promotes overall wellbeing.

2. Practice mindful eating:

Transform your meals into mindful experiences by bringing your full attention to the act of eating. Instead of eating your food quickly or in front of a screen, focus on the taste, texture, and smell of each bite. By slowing down and being present during meals, you'll encourage healthier digestion, increase satisfaction, and foster a greater appreciation for the nourishment food provides.

3. Take regular breaks from screens:

Reduce screen-based distractions and digital overwhelm by setting boundaries regarding device usage. Establish regular intervals throughout the day to step away from your devices, such as during meals or for short breaks. During these breaks, prioritize activities that foster mindfulness, such as going for a walk, engaging in deep breathing, or simply observing your surroundings without distraction.

4. Incorporate mindful movement:

Physical activities, such as walking or jogging, can be turned into mindful experiences when you practice greater awareness of your body's movement and the sensations accompanying it. Mindful movement also increases your connection to your body and helps you stay grounded in the present moment.

5. Mindful communication:

Practice mindful listening when engaging in conversations with others. Give your full attention to the person speaking, focusing on understanding their perspective without judgment. By practicing active listening, you not only demonstrate respect and empathy for the other person but also become more present and engaged in your interactions.

6. Perform daily tasks mindfully:

Bring mindfulness to mundane tasks, such as washing the dishes or folding laundry, by fully engaging your senses and paying attention to each step of the process. As you focus on the task at hand, you'll find greater enjoyment and satisfaction in these routine activities, making them more enjoyable and less of a chore.

7. Mindful breathing:

Cultivate awareness of your breath throughout the day as a simple and effective means of fostering mindfulness. When you notice yourself becoming stressed or overwhelmed by thoughts, redirect your attention to your breath, taking slow, deep inhales and exhales. This practice not only helps regulate emotions but also improves focus and concentration.

8. Meditate before bed:

Cap off your day with a brief mindfulness meditation before bed. Similar to starting your day with meditation, this evening practice can help clear your mind, release tension, and prepare your body for a restful night's sleep.

9. Participate in mindfulness workshops / programs:

Consider attending a mindfulness workshop or enrolling in an online program to deepen your practice and learn new techniques. Mindfulness courses or retreats can provide you with valuable tools, support, and guidance that can enhance your mindful living journey.

10. Establish a personal mindfulness reminder:

Choose an object or symbol that reminds you to be mindful throughout the day, such as a small stone, piece of jewelry, or even a computer screensaver. When you notice your reminder, pause for a moment to check in with yourself, assess your current mindset, and bring your attention back to the present moment.

Incorporating mindfulness into your daily life can lead to numerous benefits for both your mental and physical health. By adopting some or all of these practices and exercises, you'll create lasting habits that contribute to your overall wellbeing and foster a more mindful, intentional life. Remember, as you embark on this journey, be patient, and remind yourself that mindfulness is a practice that takes time and commitment to fully integrate into your life. Enjoy the process!

Stop, Breathe, and Be Present: Mindful Moments Throughout the Day

One of the most effective ways to incorporate mindfulness into our daily lives is to create pockets of time when we deliberately slow down, check in with ourselves, and get present. By doing so, we not only build resilience to deal with everyday stressors, but we also open up the possibility to appreciate the beauty around us, find gratitude, and experience joy – even in the most mundane of moments.

Mindful Mornings

Let's start with the very beginning of our day – the moment we wake up. Our morning routines set the tone for the rest of our day, so it's essential to start things off right. Here are a few mindful morning practices to consider:

- Set your intention for the day before getting out of bed. Take a few deep breaths and visualize how you want your day to unfold.
- Avoid reaching for your phone first thing in the morning. Instead, begin your day with a few minutes of mindful breathing, meditation, or gentle stretching.
- Savor your morning ritual, whether it's making coffee, brushing your teeth, or preparing breakfast, paying attention to the scents, tastes, and textures.
- Set aside time for a daily gratitude practice – write down three things you're grateful for each morning.

Mini-Mindfulness Breaks

Throughout the day, it's beneficial to check-in with ourselves and bring our focus back to the present moment. These mini-mindfulness breaks can help you reduce stress, improve focus and concentration, and increase overall wellbeing. Here are a few ways to incorporate these breaks into your schedule:

- Set reminders throughout the day to take a mindfulness break. Use an app, a timer on your phone, or sticky notes to remind you to take a few deep breaths, observe your surroundings, or simply notice sensations in your body.
- Take a "mindful walk" during your lunch hour or coffee break. Focus on your steps, the sensation of your feet hitting the ground, your breath, and the sights and sounds around you.
- Before and during meetings or phone calls, take a moment to notice your breath and how you're feeling. Set an intention for the conversation and remember to bring your attention back to your breath if you find yourself becoming stressed or overwhelmed.
- When you find yourself waiting – in line, at the doctor's office, or for a meeting to start – take a few moments to practice mindfulness. Observe your surroundings, your breath, and any sensations in your body.

Mindful Evenings

The way we end our day is just as important as how we begin it. By winding down with a sense of mindfulness, we can release any tension from the day, set ourselves up for restorative sleep, and start fresh the next day. Try these mindful evening practices:

- Create a digital sunset by setting a specific time each evening when you turn off screens and devices. Use this time to engage in self-care practices or connect with loved ones.

- Practice "mindful eating" during dinner. Savor the flavors, textures, and smells of your meal, and chew slowly. Express gratitude for the nourishment and the process it took to bring the food to your plate.
- Cultivate a mindful bedtime routine. Consider incorporating gentle stretching, deep breathing exercises, or body scan meditations to help you relax and prepare for a restful night's sleep.
- Keep a gratitude journal beside your bed and write down three things you're grateful for each evening.

Remember, the key to incorporating mindfulness into your daily life is to make it a habit. Start small, be consistent, and remain gentle with yourself as you build these practices into your routine. Over time, you will notice how mindfulness enhances your experience of daily life and supports your digital detox journey, leading to a more present, balanced, and connected existence.

9. Creating Healthy Digital Habits: Setting Boundaries and Maintaining Balance

Setting Boundaries and Maintaining Balance

In today's digital age, the constant connectivity and distraction from electronic devices can leave our minds feeling fatigued and overwhelmed. To protect our mental well-being and lead a more balanced life, it's vital to establish healthy digital habits. Setting boundaries and maintaining balance in our use of technology can benefit our mental health, social relationships, and overall happiness. In this section, we will explore strategies to create and sustain healthy digital habits, which in turn will contribute to a more mindful living experience.

Establish Clear Boundaries

Setting boundaries for technology use is essential to maintaining balance in our lives. Clarity in what is acceptable and what is not allows us to take control of our time and ensures that technology serves us rather than the other way around. Here are some tips to establish clear boundaries:

1. **Create a schedule**: Determine when and for how long you will engage with technology. Be intentional about your hours of connectivity and, more importantly, your hours of disconnection. For example, you could set a rule to avoid screens during meals or an hour before bedtime.
2. **Prioritize offline activities**: Invest time and energy in hobbies, interests and relationships that don't involve screens. This could include reading physical books, playing sports, engaging in artistic pursuits, or spending quality time with friends and family.
3. **Establish device-free zones**: Designate specific areas in your home, such as the bedroom or dining room, as device-free zones. This will encourage more mindful and present interactions with your environment and the people around you.

Actively Maintain Balance

Once you've established clear boundaries, it's essential to actively maintain balance in your digital habits. Be vigilant in ensuring that technology doesn't take over your life by following these tips:

1. **Monitor your usage**: Track the time you spend on different devices and apps. Being aware of how much time you're spending online can help you make better decisions about your digital habits. There are apps available that can help you monitor your screen time and even set limits for specific apps or activities.
2. **Take regular digital detoxes**: Periodically, take a break from technology for a day or even a week. Use this time to recenter yourself and engage in activities that rejuvenate your mind and body.
3. **Set specific goals**: In order to maintain balance in your digital habits, set specific goals for yourself. For example, you could decide to limit your social media usage to 30 minutes per day, or only check email three times per day. Having a clear goal can make it easier to stay disciplined in your habits.

Cultivate Mindfulness and Self-Compassion

As you work towards creating healthy digital habits, remember to cultivate mindfulness and self-compassion. Be present and aware of how technology usage affects your emotions, relationships, and overall well-being. Recognize when a digital detox might be warranted, and don't be too hard on yourself if you sometimes struggle to maintain balance. It's crucial to remember that setting boundaries and maintaining balance are continuous processes, and it's okay if they're not perfect every day.

1. **Practice mindfulness**: Be present in your interactions with technology. Pay attention to how the time spent on screens affects your mood, energy

levels, and relationships. Recognize when you might need to step back and take a break.
2. **Forgive yourself**: Like any habit, establishing healthy digital behaviors takes time and practice. Forgive yourself if you occasionally slip up and spend more time online than you'd like. Use these moments as opportunities for self-reflection and growth, rather than as reasons to berate yourself.

Embracing a Balanced Digital Life

In conclusion, creating healthy digital habits is essential for finding balance and happiness in our fast-paced, connected world. By establishing clear boundaries, actively maintaining balance, and cultivating mindfulness and self-compassion, we can take control of our technology usage and ensure that it serves us in a positive way.

Remember that setting boundaries and maintaining balance is a continuous, evolving process, and the journey will look different for everyone. Keep revisiting and refining your strategies, and be patient with yourself as you work towards a more mindful and balanced digital life.

Creating Healthy Digital Habits: Setting Boundaries and Maintaining Balance

As we continue to integrate technology into our daily lives, the need to adopt healthy digital habits becomes increasingly important. By setting boundaries and maintaining balance, we can avoid the common pitfalls of overconsumption, such as technology addiction, social media envy, and information overload. In this section, we will discuss the strategies and practices for creating a balanced digital life, which includes:

1. Establishing your digital values and priorities
2. Setting usage limits and implementing technology breaks
3. Developing mindful consumption and communication habits
4. Fostering in-person connections and nurturing genuine relationships
5. Embracing digital minimalism and simplifying your online life

1. Establishing Your Digital Values and Priorities

Before embarking on your digital detox journey, it's important to reflect on your values and priorities with regard to technology usage. Ask yourself the following questions:

- Do my digital choices reflect my personal values?
- What role do I want technology to play in my life?
- How can I use technology more purposefully and intentionally?
- What online activities and platforms bring value to my life?

Once you have a clearer understanding of your digital values and priorities, it will be easier to create a plan that aligns with these goals.

2. Setting Usage Limits and Implementing Technology Breaks

In order to maintain balance in your digital life, it's essential to set usage limits and schedule regular technology breaks.

Here are some strategies to help you regain control of your time:

- Set daily screen time limits or allocate a specific number of hours/minutes for each online activity or platform.
- Use apps like Freedom, Moment, or Forest to track your usage or block certain websites/apps during designated times.
- Disable notifications for non-essential apps or switch your phone to 'Do Not Disturb' mode during certain hours.
- Schedule regular digital detox days or weekends (once a month, for example) to disconnect entirely and recharge.
- Take short technology breaks or "micro-detoxes" throughout the day (e.g., during lunch or before bedtime) to disconnect.

3. Developing Mindful Consumption and Communication Habits

To foster healthier digital habits, it's important to practice mindful consumption and communication. Keep these practices in mind as you interact with technology:

- Before checking your phone or browsing online, pause and ask yourself: "Do I have a specific purpose or intention behind this action?"
- Make an effort to focus on one digital activity at a time, avoiding mindless scrolling or compulsive multitasking.
- Listen to your body and recognize when you need to take a break or switch tasks (e.g., feeling tense or fatigued).

- Practice conscious posting and commenting online, considering both the purpose of your message and the impact it may have on others.
- Be mindful of the content you consume and the conversations you engage in, ensuring they align with your digital values and priorities.

4. Fostering In-Person Connections and Nurturing Genuine Relationships

As our world becomes increasingly digital, it's easy to forget the importance of in-person connections and authentic relationships. Keep these tips in mind to maintain balance in your social life:

- Prioritize face-to-face interactions over digital communication whenever possible, setting aside dedicated time for social activities.
- Cultivate a habit of deep listening and genuine connection during conversations, reducing distractions and being fully present.
- Consider joining local clubs, organizations, or hobbyist groups to strengthen your community connections and forge authentic friendships.
- Participate in tech-free family dinners or gatherings to foster quality time and meaningful conversation.
- Foster a balance between online and offline relationships by integrating some digital connections into real-life settings, such as connecting with online friends through meetups or events.

5. Embracing Digital Minimalism and Simplifying Your Online Life

Digital minimalism is the practice of intentionally reducing your digital footprint and simplifying your online life. By embracing this philosophy, you can regain focus and control over your time and attention. Here are some ways to practice digital minimalism:

- Conduct an audit of your online accounts and delete or unsubscribe from those that no longer serve a purpose or align with your digital values.
- Choose a select few social media platforms or online communities to focus your energy and engagement, rather than trying to maintain a presence across multiple sites.
- Establish a digital decluttering routine (e.g., monthly or quarterly) to review and streamline your devices, apps, and digital files.
- Set boundaries for your digital consumption by avoiding clickbait articles, limiting news intake, and committing to a specific number of newsletters, podcasts, or online courses.
- Work on developing healthy offline habits and hobbies to replace excessive technology use, such as reading, exercising, or practicing a creative skill.

By adopting these strategies, you can set strong boundaries and maintain balance in your digital life, paving the way for a more mindful, intentional, and present existence. With persistence and commitment, you can foster healthier digital habits, enhance your well-being, and reap the benefits of a more balanced life.

Setting Boundaries and Maintaining Balance: A Holistic Approach to Digital Well-being

We live in an era where our days are filled with an overwhelming amount of digital stimuli. From smartphones, e-mails, social media, binge-worthy series on streaming platforms, and never-ending browsing sessions, there's an undeniable need to reevaluate the way we use digital technology. As we aim to create healthier digital habits, we also need to recognize the importance of setting boundaries and maintaining a balance for our physical, psychological, and emotional well-being.

Identifying Your Digital Habits

One of the first steps in delineating the line between healthy and unhealthy digital habits is a **thorough assessment of your present routines**. Track your day-to-day usage, download an app to track your screen time, or maintain a journal to help you document your online behaviors. Keep these questions in mind:

- What times of day are you most frequently online, and why?
- Can you identify specific situations or events that prompt you to connect?
- Are there certain platforms or applications that take up the majority of your digital consumption?

By analyzing your existing digital habits, you can better understand what needs to change, create a roadmap for your digital detox journey, and ultimately establish healthier habits in your day-to-day life.

Creating and Implementing Smart Digital Boundaries

Based on your assessment of your digital life, establish consciously constructed **digital boundaries**. Take action to implement these boundaries consistently and continually revisit them to ensure their effectiveness. Here are some strategies to consider:

1. **Define "Digital-Free" Zones and Times.** Physical and temporal boundaries can be extremely effective. Establish rooms in your home that are device-free, such as the bedroom, to create a sanctuary for rest and rejuvenation. Additionally, set times for digital disconnection, such as during meals, an hour before bedtime, or during designated "family time."
2. **Set Limits on Specific Platforms and Applications.** Social media, e-mail, and entertainment platforms are common culprits of overconsumption. Create rules for usage, such as checking e-mail only at designated times or bulk-responding messages. Commit to watching a single episode of a series per week, or plan social media posts in advance to limit reactive scrolling.
3. **Limit Notifications.** Frequent notification sounds and vibrations can be distracting and anxiety-inducing. Turn off non-essential notifications on your devices, and consider implementing a strict "silent mode" policy for a portion of the day.
4. **Opt for Analog.** Embrace analog alternatives to digital activities. Read physical books, write in a journal, or use an alarm clock instead of your phone. You may find that these analog activities provide a sense of satisfaction and soothing that their digital counterparts simply cannot replicate.

Cultivating Mindfulness in the Digital Age

While setting boundaries is a critical first step, **long-term digital well-being depends on cultivating mindfulness** in our everyday choices. Here are some mindful practices to incorporate into your digital detox journey:

1. **The "Why" Test.** Each time you reach for your device, pause and ask yourself, "Why am I doing this?" By increasing your awareness of your motives, you can more easily recognize and avoid unhealthy digital behaviors.
2. **Gratitude Practices.** Instead of venting and seeking validation online, take the time to connect with the essential people in your life through phone calls or face-to-face conversations. Express gratitude on a regular basis by telling these individuals how much they mean to you.
3. **Embrace Silence.** As we continually approach information overload, embracing silence can work wonders for our mindfulness and overall well-being. Take breaks from audio and visual stimulation, and give yourself opportunities to rest, breathe, and reflect.
4. **Digital Savoring.** Choose one positive digital experience each day and savor it. Fully engage with the content, taking the time to appreciate it entirely. Afterward, reflect on why this experience was enjoyable for you.

Conclusion

By identifying your current digital habits, creating and implementing smart digital boundaries, and fostering mindfulness, you can achieve a balanced digital lifestyle that supports your overall well-being. Remember to be patient and kind to yourself as you embark on this journey toward a healthier, more mindful connection with the digital world.

9. Creating Healthy Digital Habits: Setting Boundaries and Maintaining Balance

In our modern world, we are inundated with technology and constant connectivity. While these advances have transformed our lives in remarkable ways, they have also created a pressing need to establish healthy digital habits. By setting boundaries and maintaining balance, we can harness the power of technology while avoiding the pitfalls of screen addiction, mental fatigue, and compromised relationships.

The Importance of Setting Boundaries

The phrase, "technology has no boundaries," is commonly used to emphasize the endless possibilities it presents. However, the lack of boundaries can be a double-edged sword — if left uncontrolled, technology can quickly infiltrate and dominate every aspect of our lives.

Setting boundaries with digital devices encourages a sense of control and intention in our usage. This practice preserves time for other essential aspects of our lives, such as self-care and nurturing our relationships. By taking steps to set clear boundaries with our devices, we protect ourselves from the addictive nature of constant connection and allow ourselves to be present in our everyday lives.

Establish screen-free zones and times

Choose designated areas in your home where devices are not allowed, such as the bedroom or dining room. By doing so, you encourage relaxation and mindfulness in these spaces, allowing for deeper connections with yourself and your loved ones. Additionally, designate particular times when screens are off-limits, such as during meals, early morning hours, or before bedtime. By setting parameters, you allow yourself to develop a more structured usage pattern and steer clear from excessive indulgence.

Set usage limits

To avoid spending excessive time on devices, establish clear boundaries by defining the duration, frequency, or conditions of usage. Utilize features offered by many devices, such as time limits and app restrictions. For instance, you may only browse social media during allotted time slots or limit specific apps to a predetermined daily amount. By consciously setting these limits, you prevent mindless scrolling and help ensure that your activities align with your goals and values.

Define your purpose

Before using your device, pause and reflect on your intention: Are you seeking information, entertainment, or connection? What are you hoping to accomplish? Having a clear purpose will not only help you use technology more efficiently, but it will prevent you from aimlessly engaging with the screen, only to realize hours have passed.

Maintaining Balance in the Digital World

Even with boundaries in place, striking a balance between the digital world and our daily lives can be challenging. Maintaining this equilibrium is crucial for our mental and emotional well-being, as well as the quality of our relationships.

Prioritize face-to-face interaction

While it may seem basic, prioritize spending quality time with family and friends. Engage in shared activities and hobbies without the constant presence of screens. This practice builds and strengthens connections with others, fosters meaningful conversations and helps reduce the loneliness that can accompany excessive technology usage.

Engage in screen-free hobbies

Give yourself the gift of engaging in activities and hobbies that don't require a screen. This can be anything from cooking, painting, writing, reading, or practicing yoga. By replacing some screen time with screen-free activities, you help reduce mental fatigue and establish a more diverse set of interests to cultivate creativity and personal growth.

Break the dependency cycle

The urge to reach for digital devices can stem from the so-called 'Fear of Missing Out' (FOMO), as well as the dopamine hits our brains receive when we encounter novel information. Challenge yourself to delay checking your phone for updates and notifications — take a deep breath and sit with the discomfort. Gradually, you'll find that this dependency begins to weaken as you more mindfully engage with your devices.

Self-care and digital detox

Taking frequent breaks from technology is essential for mental and emotional well-being. Set aside time for a digital detox — whether it's for an hour per day, a full day on weekends, or a defined period during vacations. Use this time to recharge, reflect, engage in self-care practices, and connect with loved ones in meaningful ways.

Cultivating healthy digital habits is a process that requires awareness, effort, and determination. As you set boundaries and strive for balance, remember to be gentle with yourself and understand that positive change takes time. By doing so, you create a foundation that allows you to embrace the transformative power of technology without compromising your well-being or ability to live a mindful, connected life.

Establishing Boundaries for Digital Consumption

Our daily lives are becoming increasingly dominated by digital devices and online platforms, leaving us with little time to establish and maintain healthy boundaries. That's why it's crucial to deliberately set limits on our digital consumption, both to preserve our mental health and to maintain a balanced lifestyle. Below are some strategies for setting appropriate boundaries for a healthier digital diet.

1. Understand and define your values

Start by taking the time to reflect on what is essential in your life, both personally and professionally. Write down your core values and what you want to accomplish with your digital device usage. When you are aware of your values and align your digital habits accordingly, you're more likely to prevent unnecessary digital exposure and maintain a healthy balance.

2. Set specific goals and limits

Based on your values, create reasonable goals to keep your digital consumption in check. Determine how much time you want to spend on social media, emails, and browsing the internet. Set tangible targets like "no more than 30 minutes a day on social media" or "check emails only twice a day" to create purposeful boundaries.

3. Prioritize important tasks and engagements

To ensure productive use of your digital devices, identify and prioritize the most important tasks that require your attention. This approach allows you to make the most of your screen time and encourages you to engage in meaningful digital activities that serve a clear purpose.

4. Unplug frequently and consistently

Designate specific times during the day for digital breaks. By incorporating regular, structured breaks from technology (e.g., during lunch and dinner, or after a set amount of work completed), you can help alleviate feelings of digital overwhelm and maintain your focus on the present moment.

5. Establish device-free zones and times

Identify areas of your home or workplace where digital devices are not allowed, like the bedroom, dining room, or outdoor spaces. Implementing device-free zones and times throughout the day and evening encourages you to engage in more mindful and present activities, such as deep conversations, reading, or meditation.

6. Schedule periods of digital disconnection

Designate a period each week or month where you intentionally distance yourself from digital devices, apps, or platforms. This "digital detox" will allow you to reconnect with yourself and your surroundings and help you practice mindfulness in your daily life.

7. Communicate your boundaries with others

To successfully establish and maintain your digital boundaries, it's crucial to communicate these limits to those around you, such as friends, family, and colleagues. By doing this, you create mutual understanding and accountability and support each other in observing healthier digital habits.

8. Use tools to help set boundaries

Consider utilizing digital tools designed to help establish and maintain healthy boundaries. Examples include website blockers, time-tracking apps, or built-in features on your devices that help you monitor your usage. These tools can act as constant reminders of your goals and reduce the temptation to engage in unhealthy digital habits.

9. Practice self-compassion

Setting and maintaining digital boundaries can be challenging, and you might not always adhere to your own rules. It's crucial to practice understanding and forgiveness when you slip up. Accept that setbacks are part of the learning process, and use these experiences as opportunities to refine and adjust your digital boundaries.

10. Continuously reassess your needs and progress

Regularly evaluate your digital habits and boundaries to ensure they accurately serve your needs and align with your values. Adapt your boundaries as you grow and change, and as your digital consumption evolves. Continuous self-assessment allows you to remain conscious of your relationship with technology, ensuring sustainability and balance in your digital life.

Achieving a balanced digital lifestyle requires intentionality, self-reflection, and persistence. By setting thoughtful boundaries and remaining committed to maintaining them, you'll be better equipped to navigate the digital world and foster a more mindful, present, and connected life.

10. Achieving Sustainable Digital Wellness: A Journey Towards Mindful Living

10.1 Understanding Digital Wellness

Digital wellness refers to the optimal state of well-being that an individual can achieve by maintaining a healthy balance between their use of technology and other aspects of their life. As the world becomes increasingly connected, achieving digital wellness becomes a critical aspect of overall health and well-being.

The journey towards sustainable digital wellness starts by understanding how technology influences our lives and acknowledging its advantages alongside its potential negative impacts on our mental and physical health. It is important that we take a step back and evaluate our relationship with technology, focusing not just on its benefits, but also considering how it may be causing stress, anxiety, or hindering our growth.

10.2 Mindfulness: The Cornerstone of Digital Wellness

Mindfulness is the practice of paying full attention to the present moment, and observing thoughts, feelings, and sensations without judgment. It is a powerful tool to help restore balance in our lives by reconnecting with ourselves and our surroundings. Developing a strong foundation in mindfulness can help us become more aware of the impact of technology on our lives and make informed choices about how to use it.

Here are some strategies for cultivating mindfulness in your daily life:

- **Meditation:** Regular meditation helps train your mind to focus on the present moment, which can improve your awareness of your own digital habits and their effects on your overall well-being.
- **Breathing exercises:** Taking a few minutes each day to practice deep breathing or other relaxation techniques can improve your ability to cope with the stresses associated with technology use.
- **Outdoor activities:** Spending time in nature, away from screens and devices, can help you reset and recharge, while also providing an opportunity to reconnect with yourself.

10.3 Creating a Balanced Digital Life

Understanding the need for mindfulness and digital wellness is just the first step. It is equally essential to put this understanding into practice by creating a balanced digital life. Here are some tips for achieving balance and fostering digital wellness:

- **Set clear boundaries:** Create boundaries between your work and personal life, such as by designating specific hours for email, social media, and other tech use. Avoid using devices during mealtimes or a couple of hours before bedtime.
- **Practice digital minimalism:** Consider reducing the number of applications and devices you use, and focus on their essential functions to declutter your digital space.
- **Prioritize human connections:** Make an effort to engage in personal interactions, whether through phone calls or face-to-face conversations, rather than relying solely on texting and social media.
- **Schedule tech-free time:** Designate specific times during the day or week when you are completely disconnected from technology, allowing yourself to be fully present in your surroundings.

10.4 Enhancing Mental Health through Digital Wellness

The journey towards digital wellness also includes fostering mental health by proactively addressing any unhealthy digital habits that may cause stress or anxiety. Here are some ways to improve your mental health as part of your digital wellness journey:

- **Develop a healthy relationship with social media:** Limit your time spent on social media and be mindful of how it affects your mood and self-esteem. Focus on using it to genuinely connect with others instead of as a tool for comparison or validation.
- **Practice gratitude:** Regularly reflect on the positive aspects of your life, including the ways technology has positively impacted it. Gratitude can help shift your focus from potential stressors to the things that bring joy and fulfillment.

- **Seek professional help if needed:** If you struggle with your relationship with technology, consider seeking assistance from a professional, such as a therapist or counselor who specializes in digital wellness.

10.5 Embracing a Future of Continuous Growth and Learning

Achieving sustainable digital wellness is an ongoing journey that requires constant reflection and adaptation. Be prepared to reassess your digital habits and make changes where necessary, as technology continues to evolve and impact our lives in new ways.

Engaging in this journey of continuous growth will not only improve your digital wellness, but also foster healthier relationships with yourself and others, and greatly enhance your overall well-being and quality of life. Commit to cultivating mindfulness and a balanced digital life, and witness the remarkable positive transformation in how you experience the world.

10. Achieving Sustainable Digital Wellness: A Journey Towards Mindful Living

To achieve a well-rounded digital wellness, it is essential not only to focus on limiting the influence of technology on our day-to-day lives, but to also make a conscious effort in fostering a sustainable foundation that promotes mindfulness and healthier living. Here, we explore various steps and habits we can incorporate into our routines to ensure we not only achieve temporary digital detox but also continuously maintain long-lasting digital wellness.

10.1. Establishing Intentional Digital Habits

One of the primary steps in achieving sustainable digital wellness is to identify the time and effort spent on digital devices and develop habits that facilitate controlling these factors. Some suggestions for forming intentional digital habits include:

- **Analog alternatives:** Replace digital tasks with simple, analog versions where possible, such as using a traditional alarm clock rather than relying on a phone alarm, or reading physical books instead of eBooks.
- **Scheduled device-free time:** Set designated slots of time during the day that are reserved for engaging in activities without any digital interruptions, such as daily exercise routines, social interactions, or quiet reflection.
- **Mindful social media use:** Be selective and conscious in your choice of social media platforms, and limit follows or friendships to quality connections that benefit your emotional and mental well-being.
- **Establish device zoning:** Designate specific spaces in your home or office where device usage is restricted, such as the bedroom or dining area. Ideally, these areas should be conducive to relaxation, rest, or focused conversation.

10.2. Encouraging Mindfulness and Reflection

Coupling intentional digital habits with a conscious effort to promote mindfulness and moments of reflection proves to be an effective approach to sustainable digital wellness. Some techniques to encourage mindfulness include:

- **Practicing meditation:** Meditation is a valuable tool in allowing oneself to become more in tune with their emotional and mental states, encouraging a better understanding of personal boundaries and stressors related to digital consumption.
- **Breathing exercises:** Simple breathing exercises help ground the mind in the present moment, allowing for better stress management and a heightened awareness of the need for digital detox.
- **Journaling:** Putting thoughts on paper is an excellent way of processing emotions, clearing the clutter of the mind, and promoting a healthier perspective on digital usage.
- **Gratitude exercises:** Reflecting on the positive aspects of life and the riches of interpersonal relationships aids in fostering a renewed appreciation for experiences and connections beyond the digital sphere.

10.3. Nurturing Physical and Emotional Wellness

Digital wellness also depends on a wholesome, holistic focus on physical and emotional health. Some ways to achieve this are:

- **Exercise:** Incorporate regular exercise into your daily routine, ensuring it is free from digital interruptions. Physical fitness contributes to mental clarity and enhanced emotional well-being.
- **Healthy diet:** Consuming a balanced diet significantly impacts mood and energy levels, reducing dependence on digital devices as sources of comfort or stimulus.

- **Quality sleep:** Prioritize a sufficient sleep schedule, ensuring a device-free sleep environment to improve both mental and physical health.
- **Cultivating in-person relationships:** Invest time in nurturing and growing meaningful connections with friends, family, and peers, emphasizing face-to-face interaction over digital communication.

Achieving sustainable digital wellness is an ongoing process that requires consistent attention and intention. By implementing mindful habits, engaging in regular reflection, and focusing on whole-body wellness, we can take meaningful steps towards creating healthier lives both online and offline.

10. Achieving Sustainable Digital Wellness: A Journey Towards Mindful Living

Our modern lives are intricately connected to digital technology, and while this has brought countless conveniences and creativity into our lives, it has also led to a heightened feeling of disconnection from ourselves and the world around us. In recent years, people have started to pay more attention to the idea of "digital wellness," which is the practice of maintaining a healthy balance between our digital and "real" worlds. Digital wellness focuses on fostering mindful habits to help you remain grounded, maintain a sense of focus, and set clear boundaries between yourself and the digital world.

Achieving sustainable digital wellness is an ongoing and intentional journey. It is about developing the understanding, self-awareness, and discipline needed to set proper boundaries and cultivate a harmonious relationship with technology. This journey is different for everyone, as we all have unique habits, preferences, and goals when it comes to our digital lives. However, the following strategies can provide valuable guidance and support as you embark on your own path to digital wellness and mindful living.

1. Assess Your Digital Habits

Before you make any changes to your digital life, it's essential to gain a clear understanding of your current habits. Spend a week tracking how you use your devices, including how much time you spend on social media, online gaming, browsing the internet, and emailing. Assess the quality of your interactions, your level of focus during work, and even how your digital activities affect your mood.

At the end of this period, reflect on your findings. Which activities or platforms drain your energy or cause you anxiety? How much time do you spend on activities that don't align with your goals or add value to your life? Use this self-awareness to create specific, achievable goals for your digital wellness journey.

2. Set Clear Digital Boundaries

To achieve digital wellness, it is important to set clear boundaries that align with your personal and professional goals. Create a technology plan that includes designated times for using devices and times when you will be completely unplugged.

For example, you could designate the first hour after waking up and the last hour before bed as "digital-free" times, to encourage a healthier morning routine and a more peaceful night's sleep. Establish boundaries for your work life as well, such as dedicating specific hours to answering emails, taking breaks for mental clarity, and logging off at a consistent time each day to maintain your work-life balance.

3. Prioritize Meaningful Connections

Instead of viewing technology as something that disconnects us, think of it as a tool to nourish the relationships that truly matter. Make a conscious effort to communicate with people who inspire, support, and challenge you.

Incorporate video calls and voice messages into your routine to maintain deeper connections, as these methods create a more personal experience than text messages. Further enrich your relationships by seeking out opportunities for face-to-face interaction, like meeting up with friends, attending support groups, or joining community events.

4. Optimize Your Digital Environment

A cluttered digital environment can contribute to feelings of overwhelm and increase stress levels. Regularly declutter your devices by organizing and eliminating old documents, bookmarks, apps, and unread emails.

A clean digital environment can also create a more positive online experience. Pay attention to the content you consume and the people or organizations you follow. Unsubscribe or unfollow any sources that no longer serve you, and actively seek out content that aligns with your values, interests, and goals.

5. Embrace Mindfulness and Presence

Mindfulness is the practice of being intentionally present in the moment, and it can be a valuable tool for enhancing digital wellness. One practical way to embody mindfulness in your digital life is to pause and reflect before using your devices, considering your intentions and desired outcomes. Do you genuinely need to use your device, or are you simply seeking a momentary distraction?

Another approach to mindfulness is to truly engage with the digital content that you consume. For example, rather than passively scrolling through social media, actively participate in the online community by sharing your thoughts, commenting on posts, and showing support for meaningful content.

6. Develop Alternative Hobbies and Self-Care Practices

Nurturing interests outside of the digital world can help break the cycle of dependence on technology. Commit to hobbies that encourage physical activity, creativity, self-reflection, or social interaction, such as gardening, yoga, journaling or attending workshops.

Incorporate self-care practices into your daily routine and make a conscious effort to dedicate time to yourself. Prioritize activities that nourish your body, mind, and spirit, whether that be spending time in nature, joining a meditation class, or simply enjoying a relaxing bath.

7. Be Patient and Compassionate With Yourself

Like any substantial change or growth, achieving sustainable digital wellness requires time, patience, and commitment. It's important to remember that progress is not always linear, and setbacks are an opportunity to learn and recalibrate your approach.

Approach your digital wellness journey with kindness and self-compassion, celebrating small victories and reminding yourself of the larger goal – a harmonious, balanced life that optimizes your relationship with technology and supports your overall well-being.

In conclusion, achieving sustainable digital wellness is a life-enhancing journey rooted in self-awareness, intentional decision-making, and dedication to personal growth. By cultivating mindful habits and seeking balance in our digital lives, we are better equipped to thrive in an increasingly connected world without losing sight of what truly matters: our mental and emotional well-being, meaningful connections, and living life in the present moment.

Achieving Sustainable Digital Wellness: A Journey Towards Mindful Living

In today's world, our lives are heavily interwoven with technology, and maintaining a healthy digital balance is essential for our overall well-being. Digital wellness refers to the state of physical, mental, and social well-being in a digital world. In this section, we will explore the journey towards achieving sustainable digital wellness and how it contributes to a mindful and holistic lifestyle.

Understanding Digital Wellness

Before embarking on the journey of achieving digital wellness, we need to understand the concept and its importance in our lives.

Digital wellness is not deprivation: It is essential to recognize that digital wellness is about achieving balance and not complete abstinence from technology. The idea is to use technology in a way that enhances our lives without causing any harm or dominating our lives to an unhealthy extent.

Physical, mental, and emotional well-being: Digital wellness encompasses all aspects of our well-being. It is essential to ensure that our screen time and technology use does not negatively impact our physical health, mental clarity, and emotional equilibrium.

Steps to Achieve Digital Wellness

Following are some of the essential steps that can help you move towards achieving digital wellness in your life:

1. Awareness and Self-Reflection: Start by identifying and acknowledging your current digital habits, and be honest with yourself about how it may be impacting various aspects of your life. Introspection will help identify areas where you need to make improvements or cut down your digital usage.

2. Set Clear Boundaries: Establish limits for your technology use. This could be in the form of daily screen time limits or specific rules such as refraining from using mobile devices during meal times or before bed.

3. Cultivate Mindfulness and Presence: Practicing mindfulness is crucial to achieve digital wellness. It entails being aware of your thoughts and actions, focusing on the present moment, and avoiding excessive multitasking. Mindfulness techniques such as meditation or breath work can help you stay grounded amid the digital chaos.

4. Prioritize Quality over Quantity: Be selective with the content you consume and the time you spend online. Prioritize meaningful connections, valuable information, and enriching experiences over mindless scrolling.

5. Regular Digital Detox: Time away from screens helps to break free from the shackles of digital addiction, and also helps prioritize quality time with family and friends. Incorporate digital detoxes into your routine, ranging from daily screen-free hours to weekend digital detoxes or even weeklong breaks.

6. Seek Professional Help: If you find yourself struggling to achieve digital wellness and maintain balance in your life, consider seeking professional guidance from a therapist or a coach who specializes in digital addiction or mental health.

Achieving Mindful Living through Digital Wellness

By incorporating digital wellness practices into your life, you pave the way for mindful living, where you can enjoy the benefits of technology without causing harm to yourself or the people around you. Some of the positive outcomes of embracing digital wellness include:

Increased self-awareness: Reflecting on our digital habits and consciously practicing moderation brings about a heightened sense of self-awareness that inevitably extends to other areas of our lives.

Stronger personal relationships: With reduced time spent on screen, you end up making more space for quality time with friends and family, strengthening your relationships and deepening your connections with the people who matter most.

Improved mental health: Excessive screen time is linked to heightened stress levels, anxiety, depression, and sleep disturbances. By practicing digital wellness, you can experience improved mental health, emotional stability, and a better sense of well-being.

Enhanced physical health: Reducing screen time and making an effort towards digital wellness will enable you to find the time and energy to invest in physical activities and exercise, leading to better health overall.

Higher productivity: By consciously limiting distractions caused by technology, you are likely to experience increased focus and productivity in your work and daily activities. Mindful living helps you stay organized, prioritize tasks, and stay on top of your goals.

Better rest and sleep: Following digital wellness principles, such as avoiding screens before bedtime and practicing relaxation techniques, will result in better sleep quality, leaving you refreshed and rejuvenated every morning.

Achieving sustainable digital wellness is a continuous journey of self-reflection, discipline, and mindful practice. It may not be easy or instantaneous, but with consistent effort and determination, it is most certainly achievable. Remember that the road to mindful living might feature challenges, but the rewards are well worth the effort. So, embrace this journey towards a balanced relationship with technology, and create a holistic and fulfilling life for yourself and those around you.

10. Achieving Sustainable Digital Wellness: A Journey Towards Mindful Living

In today's fast-paced digital world, it's easy to get caught up in the whirlwind of technology and the never-ending information stream. Social media platforms, emails, text messages, video games, and apps all fight for our attention and time, leaving us with less energy to engage in meaningful activities or even find a moment of quiet. This constant exposure to digital stimuli can create stress, anxiety, and lead to chronic dissatisfaction. As a result, achieving sustainable digital wellness and mindful living is a challenge that needs our constant attention and conscious effort. In this section, we'll discuss ways to cultivate a healthy relationship with our digital devices without becoming a Luddite.

A. Setting Intentional Goals

Start your journey toward digital wellness by setting intentions for your digital interactions. Recognize the activities that provide value and those that are merely distractions. Sketch out an action plan on how you want to utilize each device: be it for work, communication, or entertainment, and allocate time for your digital life in a balanced and disciplined manner. Mindfulness calls for self-discovery, so recognize your personal tendencies and triggers to make informed decisions, ultimately prioritizing what's most important to you.

B. Embracing Digital Minimalism & Mindful Consumption

Digital Minimalism is a philosophy that advocates for minimizing your exposure to unnecessary digital activities and focusing on the essential aspects of your technology usage. This way, you can enjoy the benefits of technology without being overwhelmed by it. To achieve this, first, declutter your digital domains by unsubscribing from unnecessary newsletters, unfollowing unimportant accounts, and deleting redundant apps. Then, make conscious decisions regarding how much content you consume and limit your exposure to what adds real value to your life.

C. Mindful Communication

Reassess your communication habits and cultivate mindful ways to connect with friends and family. Instead of constantly checking for new messages and obsessing over 'likes' and 'comments,' establish designated communication slots throughout the day. When responding to messages, practice active listening and respond thoughtfully, as opposed to impulsively. Remember that face-to-face conversations are infinitely more valuable than virtual ones, so prioritize in-person interactions whenever possible.

D. Scheduling Digital Detoxes

Regularly practice short digital detoxes to get a break from constant screen exposure. You can start by designating specific times of the day where you disengage from technology, such as during meals or an hour before bedtime. Gradually, try to extend these digital detox periods and include longer breaks like weekends or vacations. This allows you to fully focus on meaningful activities and helps you reclaim the calm that comes with being present in the moment.

E. Creating a Healthier Home Environment

Modify your physical surroundings to support your digital wellness goals. Keep technology out of the bedroom and create a dedicated workspace to create boundaries between work and relaxation. Cultivate spaces for peaceful activities such as reading, journaling, or meditation. Designate common areas in your home where digital devices are limited or not allowed, encouraging quality time for bonding and interaction with your family.

F. Prioritizing Wellness Activities

Ensure that your digital wellness journey doesn't sideline your personal well-being. Nourish your body, mind, and spirit by engaging in activities like exercise, healthy eating, and regular sleep patterns. Dedicate time to nurturing hobbies, social connections, and self-care rituals that help you recharge and reconnect with yourself.

G. Cultivating Gratitude & Reflection

A powerful tool for building mindfulness is the practice of gratitude – it provides us with perspective and grounds us in the present. Take a few minutes each day to reflect on the positive aspects of your life, the people you cherish, and the opportunities you've been given. As you find yourself contemplating and appreciating these good things, you'll inevitably become more present in your life, helping you identify moments when technology may be encroaching upon your well-being.

H. Continuous Learning & Adaptation

Achieving a sustainable digital wellness lifestyle involves ongoing self-awareness, learning, and adaptation. Stay open to new information, perspectives, and strategies, and be prepared to modify your behaviors as new challenges or opportunities arise. Remember that there is no one-size-fits-all approach, and what works for others might not work for you. So, be patient with yourself and continue to refine your digital habits.

Taking steps towards digital wellness and mindful living will require conscious effort, time, and regular reflection. Implementing the strategies outlined in this section will not only help you reduce stress and anxiety associated with technology but will also enable you to fully experience the present moment, promoting a more balanced and fulfilling life. Practice self-compassion during your digital detox journey, and remember that setbacks are opportunities to learn and grow. Embrace this new way of life, and discover the beauty of reconnecting with yourself and those around you.

Copyrights and Content Disclaimers:

AI-Assisted Content Disclaimer:
The content of this book has been generated with the assistance of artificial intelligence (AI) language models like CHatGPT and Llama. While efforts have been made to ensure the accuracy and relevance of the information provided, the author and publisher make no warranties or guarantees regarding the completeness, reliability, or suitability of the content for any specific purpose. The AI-generated content may contain errors, inaccuracies, or outdated information, and readers should exercise caution and independently verify any information before relying on it. The author and publisher shall not be held responsible for any consequences arising from the use of or reliance on the AI-generated content in this book.

General Disclaimer:
We use content-generating tools for creating this book and source a large amount of the material from text-generation tools. We make financial material and data available through our Services. In order to do so we rely on a variety of sources to gather this information. We believe these to be reliable, credible, and accurate sources. However, there may be times when the information is incorrect.
WE MAKE NO CLAIMS OR REPRESENTATIONS AS TO THE ACCURACY, COMPLETENESS, OR TRUTH OF ANY MATERIAL CONTAINED ON OUR book. NOR WILL WE BE LIABLE FOR ANY ERRORS INACCURACIES OR OMISSIONS, AND SPECIFICALLY DISCLAIMS ANY IMPLIED WARRANTIES OR MERCHANTABILITY OR FITNESS FOR ANY PARTICULAR PURPOSE AND SHALL IN NO EVENT BE LIABLE FOR ANY LOSS OF PROFIT OR ANY OTHER COMMERCIAL OR PROPERTY DAMAGE, INCLUDING BUT NOT LIMITED TO SPECIAL, INCIDENTAL, CONSEQUENTIAL, OR OTHER DAMAGES; OR FOR

DELAYS IN THE CONTENT OR TRANSMISSION OF THE DATA
ON OUR book, OR THAT THE BOOK WILL ALWAYS BE
AVAILABLE.
In addition to the above, it is important to note that language
models like ChatGPT are based on deep learning techniques
and have been trained on vast amounts of text data to generate
human-like text. This text data includes a variety of sources
such as books, articles, websites, and much more. This training
process allows the model to learn patterns and relationships
within the text and generate outputs that are coherent and
contextually appropriate.

Language models like ChatGPT can be used in a variety of
applications, including but not limited to, customer service,
content creation, and language translation. In customer
service, for example, language models can be used to answer
customer inquiries quickly and accurately, freeing up human
agents to handle more complex tasks. In content creation,
language models can be used to generate articles, summaries,
and captions, saving time and effort for content creators. In
language translation, language models can assist in translating
text from one language to another with high accuracy, helping
to break down language barriers.

It's important to keep in mind, however, that while language
models have made great strides in generating human-like text,
they are not perfect. There are still limitations to the model's
understanding of the context and meaning of the text, and it
may generate outputs that are incorrect or offensive. As such,
it's important to use language models with caution and always
verify the accuracy of the outputs generated by the model.

Financial Disclaimer
This book is dedicated to helping you understand the world of
online investing, removing any fears you may have about

getting started and helping you choose good investments. Our goal is to help you take control of your financial well-being by delivering a solid financial education and responsible investing strategies. However, the information contained on this book and in our services is for general information and educational purposes only. It is not intended as a substitute for legal, commercial and/or financial advice from a licensed professional. The business of online investing is a complicated matter that requires serious financial due diligence for each investment in order to be successful. You are strongly advised to seek the services of qualified, competent professionals prior to engaging in any investment that may impact you finances. This information is provided by this book, including how it was made, collectively referred to as the "Services."

Be Careful With Your Money. Only use strategies that you both understand the potential risks of and are comfortable taking. It is your responsibility to invest wisely and to safeguard your personal and financial information.

We believe we have a great community of investors looking to achieve and help each other achieve financial success through investing. Accordingly we encourage people to comment on our blog and possibly in the future our forum. Many people will contribute in this matter, however, there will be times when people provide misleading, deceptive or incorrect information, unintentionally or otherwise.

You should NEVER rely upon any information or opinions you read on this book, or any book that we may link to. The information you read here and in our services should be used as a launching point for your OWN RESEARCH into various companies and investing strategies so that you can make an informed decision about where and how to invest your money.

WE DO NOT GUARANTEE THE VERACITY, RELIABILITY OR COMPLETENESS OF ANY INFORMATION PROVIDED IN THE COMMENTS, FORUM OR OTHER PUBLIC AREAS OF THE book OR IN ANY HYPERLINK APPEARING ON OUR book.

Our Services are provided to help you to understand how to make good investment and personal financial decisions for yourself. You are solely responsible for the investment decisions you make. We will not be responsible for any errors or omissions on the book including in articles or postings, for hyperlinks embedded in messages, or for any results obtained from the use of such information. Nor, will we be liable for any loss or damage, including consequential damages, if any, caused by a reader's reliance on any information obtained through the use of our Services. Please do not use our book If you do not accept self-responsibility for your actions.

The U.S. Securities and Exchange Commission, (SEC), has published additional information on Cyberfraud to help you recognize and combat it effectively. You can also get additional help about online investment schemes and how to avoid them at the following books:http://www.sec.gov and http://www.finra.org, and http://www.nasaa.org these are each organizations set-up to help protect online investors.

If you choose ignore our advice and do not do independent research of the various industries, companies, and stocks, you intend to invest in and rely solely on information, "tips," or opinions found on our book – you agree that you have made a conscious, personal decision of your own free will and will not try to hold us responsible for the results thereof under any circumstance. The Services offered herein is not for the purpose of acting as your personal investment advisor. We do not know all the relevant facts about you and/or your individual needs, and we do not represent or claim that any of our Services are suitable for your needs. You should seek a registered investment advisor if you are looking for personalized advice.

Links to Other Sites. You will also be able to link to other books from time to time, through our Site. We do not have any control over the content or actions of the books we link to and will not be liable for anything that occurs in connection with the use of such books. The inclusion of any links, unless otherwise expressly stated, should not be seen as an endorsement or recommendation of that book or the views expressed therein. You, and only you, are responsible for doing your own due diligence on any book prior to doing any business with them.

Liability Disclaimers and Limitations: Under no circumstances, including but not limited to negligence, will we, nor our partners if any, or any of our affiliates, be held responsible or liable, directly or indirectly, for any loss or damage, whatsoever arising out of, or in connection with, the use of our Services, including without limitation, direct, indirect, consequential, unexpected, special, exemplary or other damages that may result, including but not limited to economic loss, injury, illness or death or any other type of loss or damage, or unexpected or adverse reactions to suggestions contained herein or otherwise caused or alleged to have been caused to you in connection with your use of any advice, goods or services you receive on the Site, regardless of the source, or any other book that you may have visited via links from our book, even if advised of the possibility of such damages.

Applicable law may not allow the limitation or exclusion of liability or incidental or consequential damages (including but not limited to lost data), so the above limitation or exclusion may not apply to you. However, in no event shall the total liability to you by us for all damages, losses, and causes of action (whether in contract, tort, or otherwise) exceed the amount paid by you to us, if any, for the use of our Services, if any. And by using our Site you expressly agree not to try to hold us liable for any consequences that result based on your use of our Services or the information provided therein, at any time, or for any reason, regardless of the circumstances.

Specific Results Disclaimer. We are dedicated to helping you take control of your financial well-being through education and investment. We provide strategies, opinions, resources and other Services that are specifically designed to cut through the noise and hype to help you make better personal finance and investment decisions. However, there is no way to guarantee any strategy or technique to be 100% effective, as results will vary by individual, and the effort and commitment they make toward achieving their goal. And, unfortunately we don't know you. Therefore, in using and/or purchasing our services you expressly agree that the results you receive from the use of those Services are solely up to you. In addition, you also expressly agree that all risks of use and any consequences of such use shall be borne exclusively by you. And that you will not to try to hold us liable at any time, or for any reason, regardless of the circumstances.

As stipulated by law, we can not and do not make any guarantees about your ability to achieve any particular results by using any Service purchased through our book. Nothing on this page, our book, or any of our services is a promise or guarantee of results, including that you will make any particular amount of money or, any money at all, you also understand, that all investments come with some risk and you may actually lose money while investing. Accordingly, any results stated on our book, in the form of testimonials, case studies or otherwise are illustrative of concepts only and should not be considered average results, or promises for actual or future performance.

purposes only and do not guarantee that readers will achieve similar results. Individual success in trading depends on various factors, including personal financial situation, risk tolerance, and the ability to consistently apply the strategies and techniques discussed.